THE 100

GREATEST

ALBUMS IN

CHRISTIAN MUSIC

THOM GRANGER, EDITOR

HARVEST
HOUSE
PUBLISHERS

EUGENE, OREGON 97402

CCM
BOOKS

NASHVILLE, TENNESSEE 37205

CCM Presents: The 100 Greatest Albums in Christian Music
Text copyright © 2001 by CCM Books, a division of CCM Communications
Published by Harvest House Publishers
Eugene, Oregon 97402 and
CCM Books, a division of CCM Communications
Nashville, Tennessee 37205

ISBN 0-7369-0281-3

Printed in the United States of America

00 01 02 03 04 05 / RDP / 10 9 8 7 6 5 4 3 2 1

Art Direction & Design: Susan Browne; Susan Browne Design

A publication of CCM Creative Ventures [A division of CCM Communications]
104 Woodmont Boulevard, Third Floor, Nashville, TN 37205

www.ccmmagazine.com

*Dedicated to all the fans
of Christian music*

INTRODUCTION

Contemporary Christian music, as it has come to be defined by publications like *CCM* magazine, had its genesis both inside and outside the walls of the organized church as the "Jesus Movement" of the late '60s and early '70s inspired a new generation of young people—raised in the rock era—to share their faith in the language of their culture. For a brief time even major pop and rock artists were recording songs with spiritual themes, but like all fads in pop culture, it moved on, to be replaced by a more secular form of introspection in the singer/songwriter, who was later booted out of the club to make way for dance floors and disco balls.

The funny thing was, the work of the early "Jesus Music" artists laid an amazingly firm foundation that generations of Christian artists have been building on ever since. And as in those early days, that work continues to go on both inside and outside the traditional church world.

Over the past 30 years, Christian artists have managed to record an incredible body of work, and since 1978 *CCM* has done its best to chronicle the movement, tell the life-changing stories of those artists and critique their recordings. The idea to begin a series of reference-type books, archiving and anthologizing the work of *CCM's* writers and editors, was one that germinated over a decade ago, but good things do come to those who wait, and you hold the evidence in your hand today.

This book celebrates 100 landmark recordings deemed to be the "greatest" by a prestigious group of contributors. The word "greatest" was chosen very deliberately as opposed to "best," as all participants were instructed to take into account popular impact as well as that which they judged to be artistically excellent.

The basis for this endeavor was the "100 Top Albums" list published in the 20th Anniversary issue of *CCM* in July 1998, which was the result of a poll of over 30 past and present *CCM* editors, writers and industry leaders. A new panel was convened to look at the albums released since that time and allow input for earlier omissions to be re-evaluated. A new list was finally decided upon, and then came the hard part—ranking them in order of importance. That's when the gloves came off (in Christian love, of course), and the results are contained herein.

Though every attempt was made at objectivity, I'll be the first to admit that this still looks very much like what it is—a critics' poll, which is always different than a readers' poll. Still, all of us who took part in this project approached it very seriously and are pleased with the results. Very few of us would take umbrage at the inclusion of any of the albums in this list. It's oftentimes the frustration over all the fine albums that aren't here that evokes wishful thinking.

In reading and editing these essays, particular themes emerge from the various writers who contributed to this book. You will note, for example, that recordings containing songs with lyrics that addressed the broader issues of the human condition (in contrast to those strictly focusing on devotional topics) are praised widely here. Ironically, many of these same artists and albums were criticized for some of those very songs by a marketplace that has come to define itself in the narrowest of terms. This is interesting, considering some of the earliest recordings under the contemporary Christian music banner (such as Larry Norman's *Only Visiting This Planet*) set the standard for songwriting that could comment on all aspects of life from a Christian perspective.

As a result of this change in the marketplace, those artists wishing to create with a wider topical palette tended, more often than not, to record for labels whose primary distribution was for the general market rather than the Christian bookstores. More than 20 of the albums included on this list, for example, were created with that philosophic foundation.

Nevertheless, the core Christian music consumer is one who is looking for lyrics that affirm his or her faith, in lyrics more blatant than veiled, more overtly religious than poetic in its language. This is true of much of the music represented in this book, though a significant number of these recordings have pushed the envelope of the Christian market at one time or another, confronting expectations with fresh approaches that often disoriented listeners at the time of their original release.

This of course, is what true artists do. It is my belief that one of the most valuable contributions artists make in our society is to cause us to see things from a different perspective by means of their art. Sometimes the initial effect of that process is one of disorientation, which is why the bolder the art, the greater the chance for strong reactions from the public. Oftentimes the artist is greeted with anything from indifference to rejection from even his or her heretofore most loyal fans.

The disorientation is necessary, however, as the first stage in a process that culminates in a reorientation that helps us see the subject in a whole new light and think about it in ways we might not have without the artist's point of view.

One of the blessings of developing this book is the opportunity to look at these recordings again, with eyes that benefit from the perspective of time, and see the incredible contributions these artists have made, for the sake of the gospel and the benefit of the church.

We know your favorite album may well not be on this list. Such is the nature of critics' polls. My hope and prayer is that this book will make you want to listen to the albums you own in your collection with new ears, inspire you to seek out copies of those you do not own and encourage you to study and enjoy anew these created works that testify so faithfully of their Creator.

—*Thom Granger*

THE CONTRIBUTORS

Lou Carlozo is a staff writer for the *Chicago Tribune* and a music writer for *CCM*, CCM Update, acaza.com and *Christian Single*. He is also a Chicago-based record producer and cofounder of Trunstock Music Group, a co-operative of Chicago-based recording artists.

Anthony DeBarros is a journalist, songwriter and worship leader who lives in northern Virginia. He has been writing for *CCM* magazine since 1998.

Thom Granger is a 30-year veteran of the Christian music scene, with experiences that range from working musician and production work on pioneering radio and television programs of the genre to an involvement with *CCM* magazine that dates back to its origins in 1978, and includes a long stint as its editor. Currently, Thom serves as A&R Director for BMGDirect and resides in New York City.

Laura Harris is a freelance writer living in Austin, Texas with her husband and three daughters. She contributes frequently to *CCM* magazine, is a columnist at Musicforce.com, and regularly writes features and music reviews for several publications including the *Austin American-Statesman*.

April Hefner is the editor of *CCM* magazine and the editorial director of CCM Communications. She has been with the Nashville-based company since 1992.

Lucas W. Hendrickson has been writing about music made in and around Nashville for more than a decade. A long-time *CCM* magazine contributor, he has written for the *Nashville Banner, The Tennessean*, citysearch.com and is currently the senior editor of MusicCountry.com.

A native New Yorker, who still resides in Brooklyn with his wife and four children (so far), **Robert Mineo** was first exposed to Christian music when Amy Grant sang barefoot at the Grammys. To date he has put his two cents into periodicals such as *CCM, The Syndicate, Cornerstone* and *True Tunes News*, and currently writes a monthly Christian music column for local music journal *The Inside Connection*.

Wendy Lee Nentwig goes through withdrawal if she is away from her CD player for too long. Fortunately, she found a job where they actually pay her to listen to music as the editor of ccmmagazine.com.

Brian Quincy Newcomb is a pastor (United Church of Christ) and music critic living in St. Louis with his family. He's written for *CCM* magazine since 1982, and contributes regularly to the pop music coverage of the *St. Louis Post-Dispatch*.

Dwight Ozard is executive director of Tony Campolo Ministries, and a veteran commentator on contemporary culture. His essay "The Seven Deadly Sins of Contemporary Christian Music" was called a "classic" by *CCM* magazine.

Jamie Lee Rake is a freelance writer, among other things, who resides in Waupun, Wisconsin. Single, though not necessarily by choice, his writing interests encompass the world of the popular arts and cuisine, while his other interests are best inquired about discreetly.

Melissa Riddle, a freelance writer, editor and antique auction junkie, is senior editorial consultant for *CCM* magazine.

Gregory Rumburg has been on staff with *CCM* magazine since 1993. A graduate of the College of Wooster and Vanderbilt Divinity School, Gregory is an ordained minister of the Christian Church (Disciples of Christ).

John W. Styll is president of CCM Communications, publishers of *CCM* magazine, CCM Update, *Youthworker* and *Worship Leader*. He serves on the Board of Directors of the Gospel Music Association and the Christian Music Trade Association. More importantly, he says, "I have been married to my first wife for 25 years and have three big kids. And I've known Thom Granger longer than anyone else in this book."

John J. Thompson founded True Tunes Etcetera, at various times a retail store, mail-order company, concert venue and magazine. He is currently the editor of TrueTunes.com and has written a history of Christian rock for ECW Press called *Raised by Wolves*.

Besides his other "hats" (writer, editor, musician), **Dave Urbanski** is the new director of product development for Youth Specialties, Inc., a San Diego-based organization that's been providing resources and training for Christian youth workers for the last 30 years. For the previous four years he served as editor of *Youthworker* journal.

Chris Willman has been a senior writer for *Entertainment Weekly* since 1995. Prior to that he was a longtime contributor to the *Los Angeles Times*, and his writing about music and film has also appeared in *CCM*, *Newsday*, *Rolling Stone*, the *Hollywood Reporter* and other publications.

ACKNOWLEDGMENTS

Many thanks to CCM Communications—to its president,
John Styll, for giving me so many of my early opportunities
and believing in me;
to April Hefner and Gregory Rumburg, for carrying the torch so
proudly and holding it so high; and to Roberta Croteau
at CCM Books for this wonderful chance to cast a backward
glance for all of you to see.

To my wife Holly and daughters Kate, Hilary, Lauren and Alison—
for understanding, once again, the need to spend a
summer's worth of weekends in front of a computer screen,
and your unconditional love.

To the writers—I've worked with some of you for so many
years now. Your dedication to this art form, long before it
was remotely cool to be a Christian music fan, is what makes you
the best at what you do. Thanks for your hard work, great writing
and big opinions. We made a book!

To all the recording artists honored in this book—those in this
world and those already in the next one. Your music gives
me life. Your words have changed my life.

To the giver of life, and all good gifts—I thank you for mine.

one

Myrrh 1988
Produced by Brown Bannister

LEAD ME ON

AMY GRANT

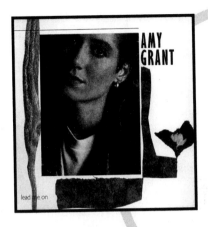

By the time of *Lead Me On's* release, Amy Grant had earned an all-access pass to the evangelical church community—the core audience for Christian music. Born in Augusta, Georgia on November 25, 1960, Grant's family soon relocated to Nashville, Tennessee, the place she still calls home. Discovered when she was 15, Grant recorded her first album in 1977. By 1988, Grant had won four Grammys and numerous Dove Awards, achieving sales resulting in six gold and two platinum albums. She had appeared on national television shows ranging from the *700 Club* to *Good Morning America, Late Night with David Letterman, The Tonight Show with Johnny Carson,* and others, and had been dubbed the queen of Christian music.

But on *Lead Me On*, Grant departed from what some were suggesting as being formulaic Christian music. She had flirted with the idea of forging new frontiers on *Unguarded*, which birthed the pop success of "Find a Way," a song which opened doors for the number one charting pop duet with former Chicago member Peter Cetera on "The Next Time I Fall."

With *Lead Me On*, Grant went all out, and in doing so unwrapped a new mirror—one larger and clearer than the genre had encountered before—reflecting something the church has always had trouble dealing with: that it, like Grant, was an awkward blend of the sacred (the stuff of God and longing for Divine presence) and the secular (of human relationships, struggle, sin and of course...rock 'n' roll).

Instead of direct references to faith and God, she altered the chemistry of her lyrics and music to explore human relationships, making this perhaps Grant's most romantic record. There is less assurance in universal truths; there is human folly and idealism woven daringly with Christian mystery, of human tragedy and finding—or not finding clearly enough—God in the midst of it all.

The original title track was "What About the Love," a prophetic Kye Fleming/Janis Ian song lobbing socially conscious inquiries toward the pious and the powerful. Through the lens of this song much of the rest of the album makes sense, exploring relationship and community as heroic (religious conversion in "1974"), tragic (temptation in "Shadows"), struggle (a lover's fidelity in "Faithless Heart"), family-centered ("Saved By Love" and "If These Walls Could Speak") and love's commitment ("Say Once More").

For this album, producer Brown Bannister orchestrated a more organic sound, utilizing various shades of acoustic instrumentation and more or less discarding *Unguarded*'s bells and whistles. The approach is fertile soil for a lyrical harvest, and functions as a reminder that though the themes are different, this is the same Amy Grant that had made popular the divine "Father's Eyes" and the warm "El Shaddai."

Lead Me On was the first Christian pop album to ship gold (at around 600,000 copies) and debuted at number one on the *CCM* Album Chart. Still, it's not Grant's biggest commercial success.

No matter. Special moments are rarely commercial success stories. Because its sound refuses to be dated, because its themes connect universally, the album stands the test of time like none other in Christian music. *Lead Me On* is a great record because it does lead those who hear it, setting a standard for creating good art. It does so not with heavy-handed utilitarianism as its whip, but with deft inquiry and challenge to the human community. Captivating as a beautiful piece of art, it lifts the human spirit—but never causes us to be so heavenly minded that we are of no earthly good.

—Gregory Rumburg

the songs

1 LEAD ME ON AMY GRANT

1974
LEAD ME ON
SHADOWS
SAVED BY LOVE
FAITHLESS HEART
WHAT ABOUT THE LOVE
IF THESE WALLS COULD SPEAK
ALL RIGHT
WAIT FOR THE HEALING
SURE ENOUGH
IF YOU HAVE TO GO AWAY
SAY ONCE MORE

two

Verve 1972
Produced by Rod Edwards, Jon Miller and Roger Han

2

ONLY VISITING THIS PLANET

LARRY NORMAN

A Bay Area-born, L.A.-based rocker who had a Top 20 pop hit with his band People! on a cover of the Zombies tune "I Love You," Larry Norman was the right voice with the right face at the right time to start this revolution. MGM Records took notice. The label signed Norman to the fledgling pop division of its Verve label, and gave Larry a real budget to make a real rock record real well. That he did.

Recorded at Beatles producer George Martin's Air Studios in London, *Only Visiting This Planet* was the manifesto of "Jesus Rock" and serves to this day to exemplify the goals, ideals and standards of everything the original architects of contemporary Christian music intended it to be.

Norman began this mission with "Why Don't You Look into Jesus," featuring a lyric more "street level" than almost anything written since, with lines like: "Gonorrhea or Valentine's Day (VD)/And you're still looking for the perfect lay/...Shooting junk till you're half insane/Broken needle in your purple vein/Why don't you look into Jesus/He's got the answer."

With big guitars and a rock gospel chorus that resembled Leon Russell's *Shelter People* and Joe Cocker's *Mad Dogs & Englishmen* (both of which, along with Dylan and the Stones, served as Norman's key musical influences), *OVTP* was underway. The album includes some of Larry's very best songs, including "The Outlaw," "The Great American Novel," a remake of his apocalyptic ballad, "I Wish We'd All Been Ready" and the anthem that would serve as a rallying cry for the movement, "Why Should the Devil Have All the Good Music?"

But the album also featured other Norman originals that would not be considered "Christian music" by current definition: "I've Got to Learn to Live Without You," a ballad about the breakup of a relationship; "Six O'Clock News," a gritty commentary on the first war (Vietnam) we watched on television; and "Pardon Me," a downright sensual song of desire in the face of sex where there is no love.

Each one of these songs is important in the scope of an album called *Only Visiting This Planet* as integral parts of society's state of affairs in the early '70s, and Norman clearly felt it important to include them along with the other, more overtly spiritual sentiments on the album. It's a lesson largely lost on many Christian artists who have followed since.

The album concludes with "Reader's Digest," a satiric look at rock culture cast in the musical mold of Dylan's "Subterranean Homesick Blues" that demythologizes many of the icons of his era. Released as a single, *Billboard's* review said it "warrants Top 40 airplay" and was the "one song on this LP that puts it firmly on the map as an album to be reckoned with."

On the original pressings of *OVTP*, there's a "bonus track" (in today's vernacular) that lasts less than a minute, but speaks volumes as Norman sings to God in a whisper: "Oh how I love you/Though words they don't come easily/How I love you/You've opened my eyes/And I can see the love that's waiting for me...."

As soon as it begins, it fades, and all of a sudden this cocky warrior is also a humble child. Before the last page of the new book of rules for this revolution is completed, Larry Norman demythologizes himself, a critical postscript to a new Christian music canon.

—Thom Granger

the songs

2 ONLY VISITING THIS PLANET LARRY NORMAN

WHY DON'T YOU LOOK INTO JESUS

THE OUTLAW

I'VE GOT TO LEARN TO LIVE WITHOUT YOU

WITHOUT LOVE YOU ARE NOTHING

I WISH WE'D ALL BEEN READY

SIX O'CLOCK NEWS

THE GREAT AMERICAN NOVEL

PARDON ME

WHY SHOULD THE DEVIL HAVE ALL THE GOOD MUSIC

READER'S DIGEST

(UNNAMED HIDDEN TRACK)

two

three

Reunion 1993
Produced by Reed Arvin

3

A LITURGY, A LEGACY, AND A RAGAMUFFIN BAND

RICH MULLINS

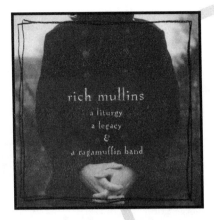

Few songwriters can consistently marry creative music and insightful theological treatise. Rich Mullins did, and he did it often. He was a singer/songwriter who first captured the attention of Christian music fans as the writer of "Sing Your Praise to the Lord" (performed by Amy Grant in 1982). By 1986 Mullins had recorded his own album and would make his masterpiece seven years later.

Inspired in part by author Brennan Manning's *The Ragamuffin Gospel*, *A Liturgy, a Legacy, and a Ragamuffin Band* explores notions of broken people in need of grace. Musically, this is reflected in the selection of studio players, gritty and rough-around-the-edges musicians like him. Produced by long-time collaborator Reed Arvin, the album features Mullins and Jimmy Abegg, Billy Crockett, Rick Elias, Arvin, Eric Darken, Danny O'Lannerghty, Lee Lundgren, Chris McHugh and Beaker, Mullins' songwriting partner, playing not only guitars, bass, drums and piano, but also mandolin, chimes, African pods, congas, squeeze-box and both lap and hammer dulcimers.

Most of the first half of the record is liturgical in subject matter, inspired by the basic words and rituals of corporate Christian worship laid out in traditional order of worship: proclamation, praise, confession, affirmation and celebration.

The understated opening of "The Color Green" finds the artist on the brink of a new day, a metaphor for the animation of creation by God. As the music swells, the majestic chorus proclaims the glory of God through creation, praising God for the amazing wonder. On "Hold Me Jesus," Mullins sidesteps historical church faith confessions, substituting instead a heartbreaking, plainspoken penitential request for divine comfort—a cry for God's relentless mercy. Mullins' imagery of one "shaking like a leaf" aptly recasts confession for a wandering community that can barely utter the word "sin." Stepping back toward traditional church liturgy, Mullins offers "Creed," his version of the Apostles' Creed made uniquely American by using a hammer dulcimer. This segment ends with a song of communion and of benediction ("Peace"). All are invited to find wholeness and meaning, dutifully serving the human community.

Of course, living out one's liturgy is another difficult matter entirely. Mullins quintessentially knew that and credibly tackles the conundrum on the balance of the album. He acknowledges the challenge of being human and being a person of faith on "Hard." Unbelievably tender is "I'll Carry On." Full of immigrant imagery, it's as if Mullins' own migratory way of life gave him connection to Ellis Island—a metaphor which importantly affirms that faith's words and practices are not the ends but the means by which one functions in the larger world. Though Mullins is poet-as-patriot on the record, "Land of My

Sojourn" makes it clear this existence is also a means to an end; that is, a season prior to being in the most desirable and holy presence of God.

Prematurely for the rest of us, Mullins got his wish when he died unexpectedly September 19, 1997. He was on the way to a benefit concert when the four-wheeler in which he was riding lost control on an Illinois highway near Peoria. Musical colleague Mitch McVicker, who was also in the vehicle, sustained extensive injuries but survived the mysterious accident. Richard Wayne Mullins is buried in his hometown of Richmond, Indiana, his liturgy and legacy remembered for ragamuffins to come.

—Gregory Rumburg

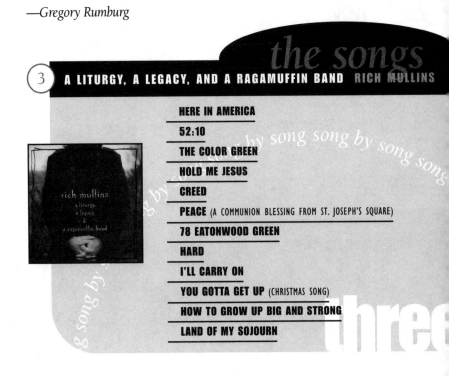

the songs

3 A LITURGY, A LEGACY, AND A RAGAMUFFIN BAND RICH MULLINS

rich mullins
a liturgy,
a legacy
&
a ragamuffin band

HERE IN AMERICA

52:10

THE COLOR GREEN

HOLD ME JESUS

CREED

PEACE (A COMMUNION BLESSING FROM ST. JOSEPH'S SQUARE)

78 EATONWOOD GREEN

HARD

I'LL CARRY ON

YOU GOTTA GET UP (CHRISTMAS SONG)

HOW TO GROW UP BIG AND STRONG

LAND OF MY SOJOURN

three

four

Fingerprint 1991
Produced by Mark Heard

4

SECOND HAND

MARK HEARD

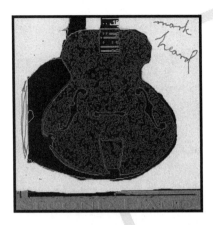

An intelligent and literate songwriter, Mark Heard assumed that his audience listened just as carefully as he wrote. Above all things, he was unflinchingly honest. When most writers panned away from questions or doubts like a camera in a James Bond love scene, Heard would remain, linger and never blink.

Heard produced a body of work in the '80s that few Christian artists could touch—eight domestic and a couple of European albums, all made on a shoestring and each of them exceptional. And then Heard dropped out. For three years he talked to general market labels about his work and discovered that they were just as frightened by his intelligence as the Christian market had been.

In 1990, he put out his own new music, releasing three albums before his untimely death in 1992 that were head and shoulders above his early work. *Second Hand* (1991) was the standout among them. With close to perfect songwriting undergirded by understated, exquisite musicianship and buoyed up by rich and memorable melodies, *Second Hand* is as good as any album released during the last decade, anywhere.

But that's not why *Second Hand* belongs on this list.

It belongs because, along with being lovely and thoughtful and perfect, it is also important. Sometime between 1987 and 1990, Heard had learned to wed lyrical economy with his piercing intellect, resulting in songs marked by tighter, less wordy, more nuanced writing that was at once smarter, more dense and also more intimate. The fact is that *Second Hand* comes close to touching nearly every major theme in western literature and Christian theology combined.

It's all there, really. Love and betrayal, the frailty of the flesh and the fleeting of the moments, our failure to love and our need for acceptance, the dogged dreariness of modernity, the desperate yearning for prosperity, justice and freedom and the nagging, lingering doubts that say it might all be a lie. And, of course, there's lots of faith, sin, redemption and hope, with even a heaping helping of a "personal relationship with Jesus"—though it's definitely of the more feisty variety.

And through every note, there's this inexplicable, overwhelming sense that this guy understands you. If Heard personally was distant and unreachable (he certainly wasn't easy to get to know), his songs at least could become your very best friends.

I remember listening to it the first time and being humbled, if a little surprised, at its ability to touch me so deeply and at its power to elicit such deep, unspoken emotions and ideas from me—genuine, human stuff that hardly ever gets acknowledged. There was—and remains—a kind of permission in *Second Hand* to be at once fearful and hopeful, trusting and tentative, to mourn and laugh and yearn and sing and actually believe that, not in spite of our frailty, but in the midst of it, God was near.

To those who insist that to be an effective witness in our culture Christian art must avoid difficult themes and be upbeat and "positive," I say listen to *Second Hand* and learn your folly.

—*Dwight Ozard*

the songs

4 **SECOND HAND** **MARK HEARD**

- NOD OVER COFFEE
- LONELY MOON
- WORRY TOO MUCH
- LOOK OVER YOUR SHOULDER
- SHE DON'T HAVE A CLUE
- TALKING IN CIRCLES
- LOVE IS NOT THE ONLY THING
- I JUST WANNA GET WARM
- ANOTHER GOOD LIE
- ALL TOO SOON
- IT'S NOT YOUR FAULT
- I'M LOOKING THROUGH YOU
- WHAT KIND OF FRIEND
- THE WAYS OF MEN

four

five

Sparrow 1977
Produced by Bill Maxwell and Keith Green

5

FOR HIM WHO HAS
EARS TO HEAR

KEITH GREEN

After a childhood stab at fame as a budding teen idol for Decca Records and many years playing the L.A. club and coffeehouse scene, Keith Green became a Christian in the early '70s and inadvertently changed the very face of contemporary Christian music. He had actually been a sort of rival troubadour of Randy Stonehill and Larry Norman back in the '60s, but once his debut record came out in 1977, Keith Green was the indisputable head of the class in Christian music.

His influence showed up early. His song "Love Broke Through" (cowritten by Green, Stonehill and Todd Fishkind) had been the title track to Phil Keaggy's sophomore effort the year before, and he performed a track on the early Sparrow musical *Firewind* called "Walk and Talk." By 1977, Green had been performing to standing-room-only crowds, and his "buzz" was unbelievable. Green's music incited a passion in his fans that was fueled by his dynamic concerts. His signatures were a percussive Elton John-style piano playing and a unique high tenor voice.

Billy Ray Hearn had left Word to start his own label (Sparrow) just a couple of years before signing Green. When the debut album was fresh from the manufacturer, Hearn packed as many as he could into his car and drove them to a festival Green was playing in Dallas. He sold every copy he brought and instantly knew this was something big. Green's momentum was unlike anything before it in Christian music. The small Sparrow staff hung on for dear life as Green took off.

The album featured the best studio performers in L.A., top-flight production by Bill Maxwell and an incredible batch of songs—each destined to become a classic. *For Him Who Has Ears to Hear* exceeded everyone's hopes and became one of the top-selling Christian albums of the day.

Despite the clearly contemporary stylings (including up-front drums and a driving band), Green somehow managed to win over even most of the ultrauptight antirock crowd. His heart was so obviously after God, and his balance of conviction with humor was captivating.

For Him Who Has Ears to Hear was the opening bell of what would be an amazing and tragically short career. In 1982, after only four original albums and one collection, Green and two of his children were killed in a small plane crash near his home in Texas. Several concert recordings were released posthumously, and Green's impact actually continued to grow well after his death.

Keith Green was definitely one of the most accomplished of the early Christian musicians. But in addition to his evocative voice and dynamic performance style, he had an immense impact in other ways. He founded Last Days Ministries, a discipleship training camp designed to equip young believers in the faith. He served as a Jeremiah-type, shaking the establishment and causing renewal and revival. His impact cannot be overstated. His songs, including several from *For Him Who Has Ears to Hear,* continue to be recorded by new artists, and several have become worship music standards in many churches.

—*John J. Thompson*

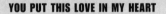

the songs

⑤ FOR HIM WHO HAS EARS TO HEAR KEITH GREEN

YOU PUT THIS LOVE IN MY HEART

I CAN'T BELIEVE IT!

BECAUSE OF YOU

WHEN I HEAR THE PRAISES START

HE'LL TAKE CARE OF THE REST

YOUR LOVE BROKE THROUGH

NO ONE BELIEVES IN ME ANYMORE (SATAN'S BOAST)

SONG TO MY PARENTS (I ONLY WANNA SEE YOU THERE)

TRIALS TURNED TO GOLD

EASTER SONG

five

six

Island Records 1987
Produced by Daniel Lanois and Brian Eno

6

THE JOSHUA TREE

U2

"I believe in the Kingdom Come," sang U2's charismatic lead singer Bono, in the anthemic "I Still Haven't Found What I'm Looking For." "You broke the bonds/You loosed the chains/You carried the cross/ and my shame/And my shame/You know I believe it." It was those words of faith and confession that connected fans of Christian music with the enigmatic U2, a brash, bold, post-punk Irish quartet that was still out to conquer the pop music world when *The Joshua Tree* was released in 1987.

Never mind that the unfinished business implied in the "Still Haven't Found" title and the record's references to drugs, human struggle and violence threw up warning flags for some. For youthful Christians living in the exile of post-modern America, U2 was a chord that rang true to their experience. Fans of Christian alternative music had already discovered the band. The Christian faith of three members had played a part on *October* and *War* (which contained a song whose lyrics were derived from Psalm 40). This time, U2 was speaking directly of the cross of Christ in a song that was garnering mainstream radio airplay. For those who had longed to see Christians receive cultural validation as artists, U2's heroic sensibility and undeniable street credibility was cause for celebration.

Musically, U2 was at the height of defining the sound they would later avoid even as hundreds of bands would pick it up. They wed an exuberant punk spirit and a tendency toward broad arena rock statements, and cascades of sound from Edge's guitar forged a path amid the more ambient approach of experimental coproducers Brian Eno and Daniel Lanois. Beyond the obvious brilliance and timeliness of the music, U2's flamboyant presence seemed near perfect on MTV, and it made them into superstars.

But in the lyrics, biblical images mixed with poetry dripping with angst and existential yearning. The language suggests many things, finally finding its beauty and meaning in the eyes of the beholder. That may explain why lyrics that enthused so many Christians failed to alienate nonreligious listeners. Like exiles, Christians and nonbelievers felt the earth groaning in anticipation of God in "Bullet the Blue Sky."

If U2 still hadn't found what it was looking for, they were learning to sing the songs of Zion in a strange land. They knew the emptiness of materialism and the numbness of drugs, and they were expressing a deeper spiritual reality. Some Christians would grow disenchanted as U2 leaned more toward irony on later albums, appearing to embrace a worldly lifestyle. But it was clear that U2 longed for the Promised Land, "Where the Streets Have No Name," and it was that yearning that connected them to so many Christian music fans. Like U2, we "wanted to believe in the hands of love" (from "Exit"), and like them we knew what it felt like "Running to Stand Still."

—*Brian Quincy Newcomb*

the songs

6 **THE JOSHUA TREE** **U 2**

WHERE THE STREETS HAVE NO NAME

I STILL HAVEN'T FOUND WHAT I'M LOOKING FOR

WITH OR WITHOUT YOU

BULLET THE BLUE SKY

RUNNING TO STAND STILL

RED HILL MINING TOWN

IN GOD'S COUNTRY

TRIP THROUGH YOUR WIRES

ONE TREE HILL

EXIT

MOTHERS OF THE DISAPPEARED

seven

Reunion 1991
Produced by Reed Arvin

7

THE WORLD AS BEST AS I
REMEMBER IT, VOLUME 1

. RICH MULLINS

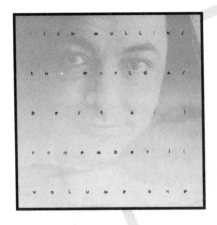

Four years *before* his first solo album, Rich Mullins' "Sing Your Praise to the Lord" (made popular by Amy Grant) was nominated for a Dove Award for Song of the Year in 1982. It was but a small sign of significant songs to come. Between his 1986 eponymous debut and 1990's *Never Picture Perfect*, Mullins had racked up four number one radio hits ("Verge of a Miracle," "Awesome God," "If I Stand" and "While the Nations Rage") and five more Dove nominations. With each new album it became increasingly clear that Mullins was made of stuff stronger and deeper than mere pop. He was a painter, a poet of uncommon insight, familiar with the rough edges of humanity and yet filled with childlike wonder.

The World As Best As I Remember It, Volume 1, Mullins' fifth solo album, painted with wide strokes the vastness and accessibility of God and His interest in our lives—invoking the beauty of nature and the truth of Scripture as colors upon a canvas. Using bagpipes, dulcimers and recorders—unheard of on "pop" albums—Mullins created sounds of wonder to reveal the omnipotence and majesty of God.

The songs here are steeped in rich imagery: "And the sky is just a bandit swinging at the end of a hangman's noose/'Cause he stole the moon and must be made to pay for it..." (from "Jacob and 2 Women"). "And the single hawk bursts into flight, and in the East the whole horizon is in flames/I feel the thunder in the sky, I see the sky about to rain/And I hear the prairies calling out Your name...." (from "Calling Out Your Name"). All are unforgettable word pictures that engulf the listener and won't let go.

Bible characters were running throughout Mullins' *World*—from Daniel, Jonah and the three Hebrew children to Jacob and Rachel and Balaam and his donkey to Esther and Jesus as a boy—another rarity in Christian pop, then and now.

"Step by Step" and "I See You," both powerfully simple choruses of praise, of seeking God's guidance, can still be heard echoing from churches and youth camps all over the world.

But Mullins saw this album, as his others, as simply "a chance to say ten significant things to those who care to listen...to share the foundational, fundamental beliefs that have shaped my life and my outlook. This *is* the world as best as I can remember it." (From the liner notes.)

Released two years after the album that delivered "Awesome God" (the anthem that would eventually represent his body of work), *The World As Best As I Remember It, Volume 1* positioned Mullins as more than an up-and-coming singer/songwriter. With this album, he became recognized as one of the most significant lyricists in Christian music. While not his magnum opus (he became a ragamuffin forever two years later; see number 3), it gave us unforgettable songs and a wide-angle-lens view of what mattered most to a poet on the verge of greatness.

—*Melissa Riddle*

the songs

⑦ THE WORLD AS BEST AS I REMEMBER IT, VOLUME 1 RICH MULLINS

STEP BY STEP

BOY LIKE ME/MAN LIKE YOU

WHERE YOU ARE

JACOB AND 2 WOMEN

THE HOWLING

CALLING OUT YOUR NAME

WHO GOD IS GONNA USE

THE RIVER

I SEE YOU

STEP BY STEP (REPRISE)

eight

Myrrh 1987
Produced by T-Bone Burnett

8

THE TURNING

LESLIE PHILLIPS

There are probably three words that best sum up the impact Leslie Phillips' *The Turning* had, not just on her career but the wider sphere of Christian music: "Dylan goes electric."

Just as Bob Dylan drew boos from former fans at folk festivals when he plugged in and rocked out in 1965, Phillips endured her share of suspicion upon making a total stylistic turnaround in 1987. In both instances, they so influenced their contemporaries that, only a few years later, even decidedly more timid artists were following in their forthright footsteps. For Phillips, it was the amplification of darker or occasionally more doubting thoughts that caused the stir, along with a shift toward—ironically—a slightly more acoustic and definitely quieter, quirkier sound. She lowered her voice, once renowned for belting and even shrieking, to a veritable and literal whisper. But it still felt like honesty at 200 decibels.

Heretofore, Phillips was the queen of Christian rock. For lack of a better handle, some secular scribes called her a Christian Pat Benatar. But she was also—as *CCM* dubbed her in an early '86 cover line—a "Smart Blonde" and a preternaturally talented pop craftsperson who could cobble together thoughtful, topical lyrics and promise an indelible hook every time. Her first three albums were full of slick '80s rock touches that seem a little dated now, but they were hardly guilty pleasures then. By Christian music standards of the time, Phillips was probably even a little bit cutting edge.

She wanted to cut deeper, and did, once Myrrh executive Tom Willett brought in legendary producer T-Bone Burnett, just the man to encourage and embellish the more personal writing she'd tended to suppress before. Phillips started recording songs about shattered love as well as restored faith. Midway through the making of the album, she decided to save most of the love songs for her next effort and keep *The Turning* focused on spiritual struggle and triumph. It told the story of someone who faces unbeatable "Expectations" and goes, well, "Down," only to accept that "Answers Don't Come Easy" and finds solace as well as a challenge in the idea that "God Is Watching You." The album was both downbeat and utterly exhilarating.

It was also a valedictory statement of sorts. Phillips' only two concerts to promote the album were performed at a Knott's Berry Farm Christian music night. Phillips' new direction was greeted with some support, but more visible were mass walkouts and much concern for her mortal soul. Her encore choice was, tellingly, Dylan's "It Ain't Me, Babe." She decided to move on from overt Christian music and sign with Virgin Records, using the nickname of Sam Phillips for her next album, *The Indescribable Wow*, which used those *Turning* leftovers and exposed her to a whole new audience.

Some viewed Leslie/Sam as a turncoat, but her impact on fellow artists was incalculable. If "honesty" is now such a buzzword in the Christian music community that it's almost a cliché, we can trace the emphasis on that quality largely back to one particular *Turning* point.

—*Chris Willman*

the songs

8 THE TURNING LESLIE PHILLIPS

RIVER OF LOVE

LOVE IS NOT LOST

THE TURNING

LIBERA ME

CARRY YOU

BEATING HEART

EXPECTATIONS

DOWN

ANSWERS DON'T COME EASY

GOD IS WATCHING YOU

nine

ForeFront 1992
Produced by Toby McKeehan,
Mark Heimermann and Joe Hogue

9

FREE AT LAST

DC TALK

There comes a juncture in the careers of great acts where one album can be called the watershed. It's the record that changes everything: the career pace, the musical focus, the level of artistry and even the band's place in history. For dc Talk—the trio of fresh young rappers who met at Jerry Falwell's Liberty University— *Free at Last* was it.

Prior to its release, the group was certainly a phenomenon; *DCTALK* (1989) and *Nu Thang* (1990) had racked up respectable sales and a growing fan base. But outside the Christian market, dc Talk was at best looked upon as a curiosity, and for the most part remained an unknown entity. With its sharply improved production values, irresistible raps and more daring musical textures, *Free at Last* (1992) not only introduced dc Talk to countless additional Christian music fans, but the mainstream music world at large. True to the disc's title, nothing would hold them back here on out.

Toby McKeehan, Kevin Max and Michael Tait had reached a point in their cojoined careers where they were ready to outgrow their status as postteen idols and become "passionate artists," to quote

McKeehan. And while *Free at Last* basically plays by the hip-hop conventions that ruled the day, it does so with abandon, joy and energy. If the albums that preceded it were a bit lightweight—and the albums that followed it were a bit heavy—then *Free at Last* showcases dc Talk at its buoyant rap/R&B/pop peak. Perhaps this image sums the album's playful spirit best: McKeehan wrote at least half the lyrics for the album while sitting in a food court at a Nashville-area mall.

Back then, the initials stood for "Decent Christian Talk," and *Free at Last* manages the nimble feat of preaching the word without sounding preachy. "Luv Is a Verb" implored listeners to treat love as more than just a feeling. Nor was love, they would declare elsewhere, a mere physical attraction. If George Michael was cooing "I Want Your Sex," dc Talk took its stand on the matter by declaring "I Don't Want It" (as in, "your sex—for now"). The song, as McKeehan would later recall, was never intended as an in-your-face reply to Michael. But the fact that it was interpreted as such only accelerated the national media attention the group was getting.

To be sure, moments of stiffness dog "Free At Last." A hip-hop cover of Bill Withers' "Lean On Me" is essentially lifted from the contemporary version by Club Nouveau, and gospel rave-ups like the title tune sound uncomfortably forced. But there are also hints of future greatness: "The Hardway" showed a new musical side of the group as serious ballad singers, and the cover of the Doobie Brothers' "Jesus Is Just Alright" not only remains faithful to the classic rock original but pumps the adrenaline a notch with its searing, guitar-charged accompaniment. The song was a head-turner for the group's loyal followers—and, in retrospect, foreshadowed the full-on rock assault of *Jesus Freak*.

—Lou Carlozo

the songs

9   FREE AT LAST   DC TALK

LUV IS A VERB

THAT KINDA GIRL

GREER

JESUS IS JUST ALRIGHT

SAY THE WORDS

WDCT

SOCIALLY ACCEPTABLE

FREE AT LAST

TIME IS...

THE HARDWAY

2 HONKS & A NEGRO

LEAN ON ME

TESTIMONY

I DON'T WANT IT

WILL POWER

WORD 2 THE FATHER

JESUS IS JUST ALRIGHT (REPRISE)

ten

Sparrow 1991
Produced by Keith Thomas

(10)

DIFFERENT LIFESTYLES

BEBE & CECE WINANS

There are many good reasons why this particular offering from the most famous brother-sister musical team of the last two decades is this list's greatest Christian R&B album of all time.

After all, it's not as though BeBe & CeCe Winans didn't have success with their self-titled 1987 debut—it featured R&B-charting hits "I.O.U. Me" and "For Always." Their second album, 1988's *Heaven*, was certified gold and became the first gospel recording since 1972 to reach the Top 10 on *Billboard's* "Hot R&B" chart. This sophomore effort also earned both BeBe and CeCe Grammys for Best Gospel Vocal Performance, as well as a Soul Train Music Award, an NAACP Image Award, six Stellar Awards and four Dove Awards.

So what's the big deal about *Different Lifestyles*? First of all, it represents BeBe & CeCe Winans' decision to pull up their gospel roots and replant them in soil rich with pop, R&B, hip-hop and jazz. The outgrowth—while still featuring BeBe and CeCe's playful, call-and-response-styled lead vocals—is a charmed, magical organism that stretches across genres and racial barriers. Second, it never hurts to do a bang-up cover of "I'll Take You There" with Mavis Staples sharing the lead vocals. Third—though it may not impress many today—any group that scored a cameo rap from MC Hammer ("The Blood") in 1991 was destined for ritzy platinum parties. And as it turned out, *Different Lifestyles* became BeBe and CeCe's first platinum-selling record.

Want more? The single, "Addictive Love," went to number one on the R&B charts, and the entire album hit number one on both the *Billboard* R&B and gospel charts, as well as nailing the Grammy for Best Contemporary Soul Gospel Album, an NAACP Image Award and a pair of Dove Awards.

Apart from the very deserved hoopla and stats, the anchor strength of *Different Lifestyles* is how unique and steadfastly listenable these dozen tunes remain. This collection appealed to music fans of many varied stripes—and for a good reason. It's not as though the duo mixed in a pop song here, a rap song there, then filled the rest of the album with R&B tunes. Instead, each song sported a unique feel and flavor, because the aforementioned musical genres were fed into each track at varying degrees. For instance, the BeBe showcase "Searching for Love (It's Real)" is dominated by his passionate, gritty, R&B-flavored vocals, but the backing track possesses a distinct jazziness. And while the MC Hammer track, "The Blood," certainly employs rap elements, the overall R&B feel is intact.

Last but not least, much of the credit must also go to producer Keith Thomas, who played every instrument on the album. (I don't care how sophisticated recording has become, it's a marvel when one person can multitrack the sound of a full, seasoned band.)

Different Lifestyles may have been Christian music's earliest successful foray into genre and racial-barrier bending, but it also opened the door at the dawn of the '90s for a ton of other artists to do the same thing, in their own way.

—*Dave Urbanski*

the songs

10 DIFFERENT LIFESTYLES BEBE & CECE WINANS

DEPEND ON YOU

ADDICTIVE LOVE

IT'S O.K.

THE BLOOD

TWO DIFFERENT LIFESTYLES

SUPPOSED TO BE

I'LL TAKE YOU THERE

YOU KNOW AND I KNOW

SEARCHING FOR LOVE (IT'S REAL)

BETTER PLACE

CAN'T TAKE THIS AWAY

ADDICTIVE LOVE (REMIX)

ten

eleven

Myrrh 1989
Produced by Russ Taff and James Hollihan Jr.

11

THE WAY HOME

RUSS TAFF

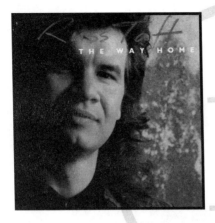

By 1989, Russ Taff had more than proven himself as a solo artist with a voice to be reckoned with. His four years with the Imperials, during which time "Praise the Lord" became a Christian music anthem, are considered the "glory days" of the legendary group, due in no small part to Taff's contribution (see the chapter on the Imperials' *One More Song for You*, number 75). In 1983, Taff made his solo debut *Walls of Glass*, a solid set of the inspirational pop of the day that showcased not only his one-of-a-kind voice but also his songwriting skill on anthems like "We Will Stand." Two years later with *Medals* (number 36), he took a giant leap into a more progressive, synth-driven rock 'n' roll that made Taff as much of a rock star as the genre affords. After *Medals* was the big shock: Taff's next release was so dark and brooding, fans and critics alike were not quite sure what to think. While sonically inventive and lyrically compelling, *Russ Taff* screamed in anguish and turmoil.

Imagine how thrilled his fans were when, in 1989, Taff released *The Way Home*, an album that purposefully expressed the end of his "long, dark night of the soul." Produced by Taff and longtime friend and collaborator, James Hollihan Jr., *The Way Home* stripped away the '80s rock sound of *Medals* and *Russ Taff* and replaced it with an organic, roots-rock approach, with the strains of traditional gospel and folk music tossed in from the artist's own roots. The album was recorded with Taff's band, live in the studio, resulting in a tangible energy not previously felt in his work. And as remarkable as Taff's voice had always been, he had never sounded better than this.

The songs on *The Way Home* are testaments to the faithfulness of God in times of trouble and God's ability to take us farther on this journey of life. The lyrics of "Farther On," a gentle ballad, speak directly to God: "I hear You have a soft spot for fools and little children/And I'm glad 'cause I've been both of those/I shook my fists up toward the sky and to most of those who loved me/A frightened angry boy in grown-up's clothes."

The Roy Orbison-esque "I Cry," as well as "Table in the Wilderness," "Winds of Change" and the gospel traditional "Ain't No Grave"—now a signature song for Taff—are all strong, honest declarations about humanity and God's grace.

In the years following, Taff's *Under Their Influence*, a tribute to his gospel roots, would release to critical acclaim and win a Grammy for Best Contemporary Gospel Album. After a Christmas album and a "best of" compilation, Taff forged a modest path into country music with *Winds of Change*—featuring remakes of "I Cry" and "Winds of

Change" from *The Way Home*. Since then, Taff has appeared on projects by various other artists and movie soundtracks, including the Grammy-winning soundtrack of *The Apostle*. In 1999, *Right Here, Right Now* marked Russ Taff's "return" to Christian music.

Finally, it is *The Way Home* that is Taff's greatest vocal achievement to date, which—given his incomparable gift—is no small statement.

—Melissa Riddle

the songs

11 THE WAY HOME RUSS TAFF

WINDS OF CHANGE

IT WAS LOVE

FARTHER ON

THE RIVER UNBROKEN

HE CAME THROUGH

I CRY

I NEED YOU

GO ON

AIN'T NO GRAVE

GUIDING LIGHT

TAKE MY HAND

TABLE IN THE WILDERNESS

eleven

twelve

What? 1986
Produced by Rick Neigher, Bob Rose,
Howard Steele and T-Bone Burnett

(12)

ROMEO UNCHAINED

TONIO K.

I was a naive student at a Christian college in 1986 when Tonio K.'s *Romeo Unchained* came into my life via our campus radio station, and it changed me forever. While there didn't seem to be much room for pain or disappointment or uncertainty in our church-sponsored youth group or midweek Bible study, here was someone who seemed to revel in discussing these topics openly.

Tonio K. eloquently lamented love gone wrong ("Perfect World"), acknowledged the fear inherent in opening our hearts to other flawed humans ("You Belong with Me") and decried the damage done by game playing ("Emotional War Games") or holding ourselves up to the impossible standards of history's supposedly great couples ("Impressed").

I had no idea back then that Tonio K. (a.k.a. Steve Krikorian) had already built a name for himself in the mainstream music world or that his moniker was taken from the Thomas Mann novella *Tonio Kröger*. I knew nothing of his previous projects *Life in the Foodchain* and *Amerika* that had reviewers dubbing him one of the angriest young men in rock (based on venomous rants like "H-A-T-R-E-D"). Like many other Christians who came upon *Romeo Unchained* through Word's What? Records (it was the imprint's inaugural release), I was completely unaware of the caustic vitriol that previously characterized Tonio K.'s work. I would only later learn that in the time between those releases and *Romeo*, Tonio had found not just a faith in God, but faith in the possibility of romance as well. As proof, shortly after the album was released the singer took the uncharacteristically optimistic step of marrying the photographer who shot the album's cover.

While *Romeo* did showcase a kinder, gentler Krikorian, some Christian DJs deemed his songs "too negative" to play. Never mind that MTV's elder statesman Kurt Loder, then writing for *Rolling Stone*, said he was tempted "to trumpet *Romeo Unchained* as the best Bob Dylan album since Dylan himself lost interest in the pop-song form." In the end Loder settled for proclaiming Tonio K. "an arousing original."

Perhaps he was a little *too* original for the '80s Christian music scene. Still, with the help of T-Bone Burnett, Charlie Sexton and David Mansfield on stringed things, Tonio K. released another album on What? called *Notes from the Lost Civilization,* but you had to buy the A&M version to get the supposedly controversial tenth track, "What Women Want." In retrospect, that was a portent of things to come. Tonio K.'s third collection of songs for the label languished for years in some back room gathering dust before finally being released in 1997 by Gadfly Records. The long-awaited "lost" album, *Olé,* featuring Paul Westerberg, Charlie Sexton and Bruce Thomas of the

Attractions was worth the wait musically, but it was a project whose time had past. Krikorian had moved on long ago.

More than anything else, Tonio K. was a realist, so he couldn't have been too surprised that he wasn't embraced wholeheartedly by all of Christian music. But what a different place it might be today if he'd been encouraged to stick around.

—*Wendy Lee Nentwig*

the songs

(12) ROMEO UNCHAINED TONIO K.

TONIO K.
Romeo Unchained

TRUE CONFESSIONS

PERFECT WORLD

ROMEO AND JANE

YOU BELONG WITH ME

IMPRESSED

I HANDLE SNAKES

EMOTIONAL WAR GAMES

LIVING DOLL

YOU DON'T BELONG HERE

YOU WILL GO FREE

twelve

thirteen

Solid Rock 1976
Produced by Larry Norman

(13)

WELCOME TO PARADISE

RANDY STONEHILL

By the time Randy Stonehill's major label debut came out in 1976, the singer/songwriter with the zany sense of humor was already well known to Christian pop concert fans. Dedicated collectors of early Christian rock, already used to tracking down Larry Norman's *Street Level* and *Bootleg* recordings, were familiar with Stonehill's hard-to-find first indie release, *Born Twice* (1970), a homemade effort by a talented newcomer.

Still, *Welcome to Paradise* arrived in a Christian subculture that held rock 'n' roll in suspicion. While Norman and Randy Matthews had produced solid, creative efforts of artful Christian pop and rock, they were ignored by Christian radio and met with opposition at every turn. So, when Solid Rock (Norman's artist-run imprint) appeared, it felt like the people who understood and loved rock music would finally be in a position to ensure the integrity of their work. To the gatekeepers of the time, it may have felt like the lunatics were running the asylum.

As such, *Welcome to Paradise* is one of the first pop/rock albums by a Christian that sounded authentic to its generation. But more importantly, Stonehill was allowed to write in a more personal, culturally relevant and down to earth manner. On *Paradise*, Stonehill wrote about complex human experiences and shared the news of God's amazing grace through poetic metaphors at a time when most Christian music felt like gospel songs with a beat, or evangelical tracts put to music.

WTP's first side was presented in a way that would attract nonbelievers, whereas the more straightforward and uplifting songs of faith were on side two. "Keep Me Runnin'" and "The Winner (High Card)" are two songs that, dealing with the lives of persons outside of the shelter of God's care without an attempt to offer a conversion or resolution, would never have appeared on a Christian album before this record.

Side one opened with "King of Hearts," a signature piece for Stonehill, his bright acoustic fingerpicking style, delicate vocal melody and profound images of a God who has created a home for humanity. It closed with "Puppet Strings," offering up another colorful look at the way sin works to break our relationship to the Creator, and how God's love provided a way for Jesus to bring us back.

"First Prayer" opened side two, moving Stonehill's protagonist toward belief in God, which led into the celebration of the birth into faith in "News for You." Two more songs stretched the lyrical limits of the times: "Lung Cancer," a fun rocker, which served only to mock smokers and hold the threat of ill-health in front of them, and "Song for Sarah," a straightforward love song that manages to include the salvation story, too.

Stonehill, a natural songwriter and singer, has delivered a catalog of fine work. However, he is best remembered for this album and these songs, and for good reason.

—*Brian Quincy Newcomb*

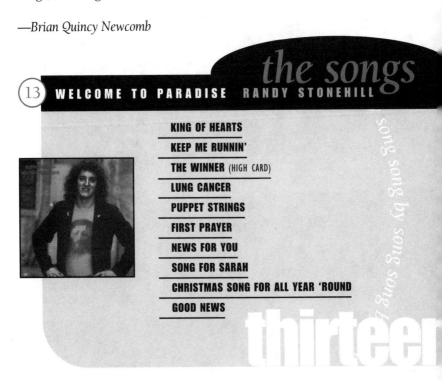

the songs

13   WELCOME TO PARADISE   RANDY STONEHILL

KING OF HEARTS

KEEP ME RUNNIN'

THE WINNER (HIGH CARD)

LUNG CANCER

PUPPET STRINGS

FIRST PRAYER

NEWS FOR YOU

SONG FOR SARAH

CHRISTMAS SONG FOR ALL YEAR 'ROUND

GOOD NEWS

thirteen

fourteen

ForeFront 1995
Produced by Toby McKeehan, Mark Heimermann
and John Painter

14

JESUS FREAK

DC TALK

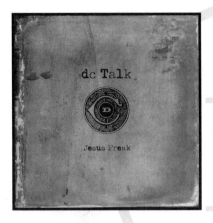

14

One of the most anticipated records of the 1990s came in the form of the eclectic and extraordinary *Jesus Freak*. The album once again raised the creative bar sonically and lyrically in Christian music, and gracefully perpetuated the rising social consciousness of the genre. In short, the 1995 release was a watershed moment for dc Talk and Christian music alike, as *Jesus Freak* constructed a walking bridge between Christian and general market music.

Almost three years had passed since dc Talk released *Free at Last* (1992), the album that showcased the group at the top of its pop/hip-hop game. *Jesus Freak* ended that era and introduced a new dc Talk, one that embraced not only its racial diversity as it had on the group's previous three albums, but also the diverse musical influences of its three front men, Toby McKeehan, Michael Tait and Kevin Max. Fans freaked over the project, eventually pushing sales to more than platinum status.

Crunchy, modern rock guitars, aggressive pop vocals and introspective and melodic ballads—not to mention occasional rapid-fire rap or spoken-word interludes—brought to life dc Talk's most intelligent lyrics, and most cohesive album, to date. Always an undercurrent in its music, the group brought to the surface its musical diversity. In less capable hands, melding modern rock, smooth midtempo pop songs and rap could have yielded an uneven listening experience. But with the group's visionary McKeehan and veteran producer Mark Heimermann at the helm, dc Talk's musical diversity created a sonic melting pot of Ellis Island proportions.

Kevin Max and Michael Tait warmed the studio microphone with rich lead vocals, giving voice to group-written lyrics of fresh religious and social poetry. Max's unique, shimmering voice and Tait's strong but smooth R&B-influenced presence lifted the group's pop sensibilities to new heights.

Although the group had significantly changed the landscape of its sound, it lost no ground in expressing lyrics of Christian concerns. Seemingly to reiterate its faithful position, the album title was a clear reference to hippie followers of Jesus Christ from a generation before, curiously asking the question, "What will people think when they hear that I'm a Jesus freak?" If that didn't assure fans of the trio's position, a dynamic cover of Charlie Peacock's confessional "In the Light" certainly did. "Colored People" joined hits like "Walls" and "Free at Last" in dc Talk's catalogue of Martin Luther King-inspired social commentary. "Day by Day," the trio's aggressive reinterpretation of the popular tune from the Broadway musical *Godspell*, simultaneously portrayed the group's religiosity and cultural savvy.

"Mind's Eye," a cut that dared to reimagine personal Christian faith by observing elements of the natural world without tired metaphors or questionable theology, sampled inquiring, spoken-word God-talk from the Reverend Billy Graham. It was one of many production elements utilized as springboards to creating a multimedia-frenzied live experience when the group toured.

With *Jesus Freak*, dc Talk went on to win more Dove Awards and Grammys, success that contributed to the group's signing with general market label partner Virgin Records, effectively widening the walking bridge this project had already created between very different music markets.

—*Gregory Rumburg*

the songs

14 JESUS FREAK   DC TALK

SO HELP ME GOD

COLORED PEOPLE

JESUS FREAK

WHAT IF I STUMBLE?

DAY BY DAY

MRS. MORGAN

BETWEEN YOU AND ME

LIKE IT, LOVE IT, NEED IT

JESUS FREAK (REPRISE)

IN THE LIGHT

WHAT HAVE WE BECOME

MIND'S EYE

ALAS MY LOVE (HIDDEN TRACK)

fifteen

Sparrow 1991
Produced by Charlie Peacock and Rick Will

15

LOVE LIFE

CHARLIE PEACOCK

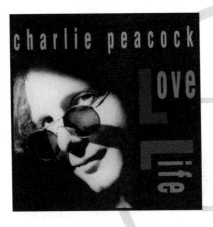

Christians may make love, but as Charlie Peacock found out with this 1991 release, talking about it is an entirely different matter. The follow up to *The Secret of Time* (number 26 on this list), *Love Life* spoke candidly—but tastefully—about relationships, primarily those between husbands and wives. From the cautionary "Another Woman in Tears" to the celebration of married love that is "After Lovin' You" to the steamy "Kiss Me Like a Woman," Peacock spoke truth in a way we had rarely heard on Christian radio. To say some weren't quite ready for the (in retrospect) rather tame honesty of *Love Life* is an understatement, but Peacock politely pointed critics to the Song of Solomon as a justification.

That's not to accuse Peacock of only having one thing on his mind. He artfully addressed spiritual love on the beautifully simple "When I Stand with You" and the aptly titled "There Was Love." He also penned an ode to hope called "I Would Go Crazy" and wrestled with his will on "In the Light" and "Forgiveness," addressing the questions inherent in Christianity at a time when others played it safe by providing only easy answers (and often garnering greater airplay).

Listening to *Love Life* in light of the current music scene makes Peacock's brilliance even more apparent—and the fact that this music was overshadowed to some degree by lyrical controversy even more tragic. It's obvious, too, that Peacock, who also served as producer with the help of Rick Will, sure knew how to spot talent. Just listen to the haunting background vocals of the late Vince Ebo and the musical mastery of Tommy Sims and future Ragamuffins Aaron Smith and Jimmy Abegg.

These days Peacock, who is slowly transitioning back to using his given (and more fitting) surname of Ashworth, is rarely found in front of the mike. That doesn't mean the singer/songwriter/producer has trouble filling his time. He's kept busy producing other people's records, including Twila Paris' *True North*, Sarah Masen's self-titled debut on his Re:Think label and work by Rich Mullins, Bob Carlisle, Al Green, Phil Keaggy and at least a dozen more. In addition, he's penned songs for everyone from Amy Grant ("Every Heartbeat") and Margaret Becker to Avalon and Audio Adrenaline.

He also seems eager to help shape the future of the industry he's been such a part of. This shows in the way he freely shares what he's learned with up-and-comers like The Normals, whom he recently mentored through the recording process, and in his first book, 1999's *At the Crossroads: An Insider's Look at the Past, Present, and Future of Contemporary Christian Music*. And you can be sure that all of Peacock's "side jobs" have had an influence on the kind of music he makes now. His tenth and latest project, *Kingdom Come*, is less a stand-alone album and more a companion piece to his book. Then again, all of his art seems somehow intertwined—each piece serving as just another medium to get across his message of living artfully and honestly.

—*Wendy Lee Nentwig*

the songs

(15) LOVE LIFE   CHARLIE PEACOCK

AFTER LOVIN' YOU
WHAT'S IT LIKE IN YOUR WORLD?
FORGIVENESS
PERSONAL REVOLUTION
ANOTHER WOMAN IN TEARS
IN THE LIGHT
THERE WAS LOVE
I WOULD GO CRAZY
KISS ME LIKE A WOMAN
WHEN I STAND WITH YOU

fifteen

sixteen

Columbia 1979
Produced by Jerry Wexler and Barry Beckett

(16)

SLOW TRAIN COMING

BOB DYLAN

How ironic is it that one of the most revered contemporary Christian music albums of all time came from a pop superstar and a secular record company? Though it was certainly shrouded in controversy on both sides of the Christian/secular divide, *Slow Train Coming* was the talk of both industries when it was released in 1979.

Following his *Rolling Thunder Review* tour (which included T-Bone Burnett in its lineup), Dylan had spent considerable time investigating the Christian faith. He had been reading the Bible for over a decade and had found its stories and lessons challenging. The songwriter accepted Christ as his Savior in 1978 and immediately began writing songs about it. His famous ability to turn a phrase, or make a simple-sounding lyric resonate with depth and truth, was never more fully realized than on *Slow Train Coming*. Though many Christians exulted at the news that "Bob Dylan got saved," the rest of the world wasn't so thrilled. Fans protested, critics jeered and audiences booed as Dylan attempted to offer some of the answers he had previously said were "Blowin' in the Wind"—and played none of his older songs in concert for the tour. Nonetheless, history has shown

Slow Train to be one of the artist's bestselling albums (it was certified platinum less than a year after its release) and earned him a Grammy for Best Gospel Album.

Slow Train opens with the now-classic R&B groove of "Gotta Serve Somebody," a decidedly bold opening salvo for this statement-of-faith album. "It may be the devil," he proclaimed more plainly than almost anything that preceded it, "or it may be the Lord, but you're gonna have to serve somebody." With the Muscle Shoals Horns providing smooth bursts of Memphis soul and the impeccably slick and emotional lead guitar licks by Dire Straits front man Mark Knopfler, Dylan was at his most accessible and enjoyable. The sonic tone established on "Gotta Serve Somebody" is faithfully maintained through the album's eight remaining tunes. In fact, with the possible exception of his late-'90s album *Time Out Of Mind*, *Slow Train* may be Dylan's most cohesive, accessible and enduring album in his impressive repertoire.

Lyrically, every song is a heartfelt and sincere discussion of the basics of Christian faith. Even the love song "Precious Angel" focuses on the singer's desire for the nonbelieving subject of the song to come around. Songs like "I Believe in You" and the title track stand as artistic high-water marks of faith in art. Few Christian artists have been able to craft such plaintive and believable songs as these first fruits of a new believer.

Slow Train Coming remains a top seller in the Christian and secular markets. It ushered in a brief but storied phase of Dylan's career in which he cranked out two additional "Christian" records (1980's *Saved* and 1981's *Shot of Love*) before returning to his more oblique, but still faithful, songwriting style. With amazing production, Dylan's extra effort at singing clearly and on key, and lyrics that wrap around the mind like a warm quilt, *Slow Train* remains one of the most important releases in pop and Christian music history.

—*John J. Thompson*

the songs

(16) **SLOW TRAIN COMING   BOB DYLAN**

SLOW TRAIN COMING
BOB DYLAN

GOTTA SERVE SOMEBODY

PRECIOUS ANGEL

I BELIEVE IN YOU

SLOW TRAIN

GONNA CHANGE MY WAY OF THINKING

DO RIGHT TO ME BABY (DO UNTO OTHERS)

WHEN YOU GONNA WAKE UP

MAN GAVE NAMES TO ALL THE ANIMALS

WHEN HE RETURNS

sixtee

seventeen

ABC/Dunhill 1974
Produced by Michael Omartian

(17)

WHITE HORSE

MICHAEL OMARTIAN

After arriving in L.A. in the early '70s from the Midwest (where he produced and cowrote an album for Campus Crusade's Armageddon Experience), Michael Omartian began making a name for himself as a session player for the likes of Steely Dan and Loggins & Messina. He went on to become a producer for artists such as Christopher Cross, Whitney Houston, Rod Stewart, Donna Summer, Vince Gill and a host of others. In fact, he is credited as being the first producer in recording history to have number one songs in three separate decades—the '70s, '80s and '90s.

White Horse came seemingly out-of-the-blue at a time when contemporary Christian music—still in its infancy—was sorely lacking in production quality (with notable exceptions). Keep in mind that this was the post-Jesus Movement era, and the general market was still releasing a few "Christian" songs and albums, but with often-dubious spiritual foundations (for example, "Spirit in the Sky").

On first glance, Omartian's album looked like it might be another quasi-spiritual attempt by a general market label to capitalize on the religious *zeitgeist*. But upon closer examination, it became clear that Omartian truly "got it," as evidenced by the lyrics of songs like "Jeremiah," "Take Me Down" and "White Horse" (all of which were penned by his wife, Stormie).

After hearing the first ten seconds of the album's opener, "Jeremiah" (later covered by Russ Taff), it was obvious that this album was different from all others that had come before. *White Horse* exhibited a level of musical sophistication rarely heard at the time, especially in Christian music.

Long, jazz-rock instrumental breaks, driven by synthesizers and horns make the album seem longer than its 32 minutes. (The title track, which seems like it would be perfect for any of the many apocalyptic movies' soundtracks, clocks in at over seven minutes.)

Stormie Omartian's crafted lyrics managed to communicate biblical ideas without the religious code that can alienate or confuse non-Christian listeners. For example, while Scripture might say, "What does it profit a man to gain the world but lose his soul," Stormie says, "Fat City, I could be livin' in/In Fat City, I could be sittin' real pretty/But it wouldn't mean a thing without you."

And check out Stormie's take on the sacrament of baptism: "Seems like yesterday when I was crying/Take me down/See me dying/He said there's life in what you do/And that's all I ask of you" ("Take Me Down").

The album is a landmark in the history of pop music made by Christians, a shining example of what can happen when top-notch music, creative lyrics and some of the best players in the world come together. It set the bar to a level that few would ever reach.

Omartian followed up *White Horse* with the incredible but lesser-known *Adam Again*, recorded for ABC/Dunhill but never released to the mainstream. Word's Myrrh label got it into the Christian market in 1975, but today both, like so many others in this book, are currently out of print.

—*John W. Styll*

the songs

(17) WHITE HORSE MICHAEL OMARTIAN

JEREMIAH
FAT CITY
THE ORPHAN
SILVER FISH
ADD UP THE WONDERS
TAKE ME DOWN
RIGHT FROM THE START
THE REST IS UP TO YOU
WHITE HORSE

song by song song by song

seventee

eighteen

Sparrow 1984
Produced by Jonathan David Brown

(18)

MELTDOWN

STEVE TAYLOR

Some may have dismissed him as just clowning around on *I Want to Be a Clone*, his debut mini-LP for Sparrow Records, but *Meltdown* proved former youth pastor Steve Taylor had a serious gift for satire, and we'd all be wise to sit up and take notice.

Making the move toward less trendy production tricks that made *Clone's* music seem dated long before its lyrics, *Meltdown* showed a new maturity. That's not to say Taylor had forgotten how to have fun. A trip to London's Madame Tussaud's led to the title track "Meltdown," with the renowned wax museum smartly serving as a metaphor for Judgment Day. Taylor then directed his biting wit at Bob Jones University's racist dating policy with the song "We Don't Need No Colour Code." Next he skewered the media for their lack of interest in accurately reporting religion with "Meat the Press."

Taylor then turned his sharp gaze on the rest of us. "Sin for a Season" went beyond the safe subject of forgiveness, reminding us that while God promises to wipe away our misdeeds if only we ask, the consequences of our actions aren't as easy to erase. With "Guilty by

Association," Taylor touched on a debate that still rages in Christian music (and Christendom at large) to this day, especially with many Christian labels and other companies having been bought up by secular big business in recent years.

The best illustration, though, of just how far Taylor had come since *Clone* was probably "Baby Doe," a chilling tale of the battle an Indiana couple fought for their Down's Syndrome-afflicted baby boy to be allowed to starve to death. While he'd taken on political issues before, the difference here was Taylor wasn't just pointing a finger at others, he was taking the blame, too. And on the haunting "Hero" Taylor got personal, recalling one of the realizations that helps hurry childhood's end, the truth that when we idolize frail, flawed humans, we're bound to be disappointed. He then went on to declare Jesus the one hero he knows he can count on without coming off sounding preachy or cliché—quite a feat.

Not all *Meltdown's* tunes have aged as well. The synth-pop sound and studio effects of "Am I in Sync?" seem particularly dated, but for such an up-to-the-minute album, it's amazing so much of the music still holds up.

In the years that followed, Taylor never lost his edge. Going on to record *On the Fritz* and *I Predict 1990* as well as a live album, he also served as lead singer for the MCA band Chagall Guevara and returned to solo recording with 1994's *Squint*, which spawned, among other things, a six-song video shot in exotic locales.

Squint is also the name he gave the label he now runs under the umbrella of Word Entertainment. Taylor is also working on a film, allowing his creativity to take new form, and he hasn't ruled out the possibility of taking another turn in front of the mike. Always growing and stretching himself, Christian music's one-time Clown Prince is seamlessly morphing into this industry's own King of All Media.

—*Wendy Lee Nentwig*

the songs

18 MELTDOWN STEVE TAYLOR

MELTDOWN (AT MADAME TUSSAUD'S)
WE DON'T NEED NO COLOUR CODE
AM I IN SYNC?
MEAT THE PRESS
OVER MY DEAD BODY
SIN FOR A SEASON
GUILTY BY ASSOCIATION
HERO
JENNY
BABY DOE

eighteen

Squint 1997
Produced by Steve Taylor

19

SIXPENCE NONE THE RICHER

SIXPENCE NONE THE RICHER

Sixpence None the Richer emerged onto the national music scene from Texas in 1992, building its reputation as a smart, female-fronted modern rock band. Despite 1995's *This Beautiful Mess*, a critically acclaimed and Dove Award-winning album produced by Armand John Petri, the band remained a cult favorite until a simple request for a kiss brought bounty to the members of Sixpence.

The story of the third, self-titled blockbuster album from Sixpence None the Richer understandably spins from the hit single, "Kiss Me." The love song was the number one pop song in the United States for two weeks and MTV's number one video in May of 1999. Extensive television support, including VH1, MTV, M2, The Box and the Fox Network's *Dawson's Creek*, plus placement in the Miramax film *She's All That*, made this underrated Christian-market band a Grammy-nominated household name.

What often gets lost in the story about the "one-hit wonder" band is that *Sixpence None the Richer* is a great album.

Produced by Christian music veteran Steve Taylor, the mood of *Sixpence* tends to be brooding and introspective, but because the songs are sensitive and delicately textured, the album avoids being dark; it's a cloudy day giving way to bursts of red-orange sky just before twilight.

Principle players Matt Slocum (guitar, cello), Leigh Nash (vocals), Dale Baker (drums) and J. J. Plasencio (bass) are at the top of their game on the recording. Woven together are warm acoustic and jangly electric guitars married with strong-yet-understated rhythms, creating complex adult pop music. It's a comfortable place for the listener to encounter Nash's bright and confident vocal style, interpreting each song as if it were her own (though only "Easy to Ignore" is penned by her). Arranged by Slocum, soaring strings accent the drama on several tracks while B-3, accordion, pedal steel and trumpet also help color the arrangements.

Lyrically, the album is a diary of sorts, largely written while the band was in flux, but more universally ruminating on finding God in troubling, even disillusioning, times. The opening trilogy—"We Have Forgotten," "Anything" and "The Waiting Room"—poignantly communicates the band's fear, frustration and doubt regarding its future, wondering—even pleading—for God's presence to be known. "Sister, Mother" was inspired by the Book of Proverbs, while "The Lines of My Earth" laments artful inspiration complicated by business concerns.

Originally the final track of *Sixpence,* "Moving On," with its repeated line "I will not let them ruin me," ties off the hopeful thread deftly stitched throughout the record. After its general market success with

"Kiss Me," the band returned to the studio to record a cover of the La's "There She Goes" (from its live repertoire) as a follow-up radio single. The cut was tacked on as a 13th track to later pressings of the CD. Its catchy melody further communicates hope and joy.

Plasencio left the band shortly after finishing the record and never toured *Sixpence*. Eventually Justin Caray (bass) and Sean Kelly (guitar) were added to the group's lineup for two years of continuous touring and public appearances.

—Gregory Rumburg

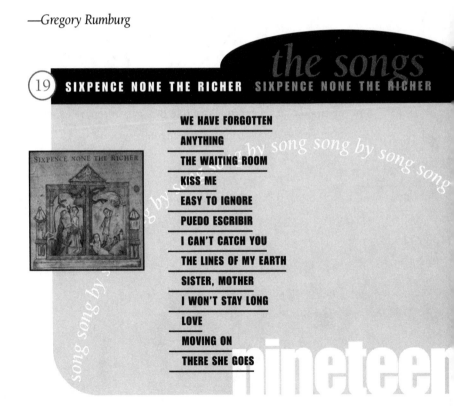

the songs

(19) SIXPENCE NONE THE RICHER   SIXPENCE NONE THE RICHER

WE HAVE FORGOTTEN

ANYTHING

THE WAITING ROOM

KISS ME

EASY TO IGNORE

PUEDO ESCRIBIR

I CAN'T CATCH YOU

THE LINES OF MY EARTH

SISTER, MOTHER

I WON'T STAY LONG

LOVE

MOVING ON

THERE SHE GOES

nineteen

Word 1993
Produced by L. Arthur Nichols

20

CRIMSON AND BLUE

PHIL KEAGGY

A matchless, legendary guitarist, seriously underrated vocalist and songwriter, beloved and consistently humble ambassador for Jesus, true pioneer—Phil Keaggy is among the most important figures in the history of Christian music.

He first showcased his uncanny, inspired guitar work in the early '70s as part of a progressive rock trio called Glass Harp. (Significantly, the Ohio-based rock band's 1970 self-titled debut is lyrically influenced by Keaggy's coinciding conversion to Christianity.) But despite Glass Harp's critical acclaim and admirable cult following, Keaggy left in 1972 after the band's third (and final) album so that he could devote his playing and singing completely to the things of the Spirit. His subsequent live shows were immediate hits—full of playful, raw improvisation and extended renditions of original tunes that grew in popularity with every gig.

But the confines of the recording studio—and the accompanying commercial demands of label suits and ties—never afforded Keaggy the springboard to reach the heights of abandon his live shows habitually attained. What's more, he literally jumped genres from recording to recording. His solo debut, *What a Day* ('73), is pure acoustic folk; the follow-up, *Love Broke Thru* ('76), is lavish, lush pop; *Emerging* ('77) is full of smooth, polyester-clad tunes; *The Master and the Musician* ('79) is experimental-instrumental; *Ph'lip Side* ('80), *Town to Town* ('81), *Play Thru Me* ('82) and *Getting Closer* ('84) are decidedly jazz infused; *Way Back Home* ('86) is a return to his folk roots; his acclaimed second instrumental effort, *The Wind and the Wheat* ('87), returns to jazz styles; *Sunday's Child* ('88) and *Find Me in These Fields* ('90) reach back to pop-rock; and *Beyond Nature* ('91) is Keaggy's first all-acoustic instrumental foray.

But with the release of 1993's *Crimson and Blue*, Keaggy hit his highest commercial and critical peak, bringing together unabashed Fab Four-influenced tuneage ("Everywhere I Look," "Love Divine"), a Van Morrison cover ("When Will I Ever Learn to Live in God"), and *finally* some bluesy, tough, extended jams that capture his in-concert energy more closely than any of his previous studio efforts. And his organic, crackerjack band (Lynn Nichols/guitar, Phil Madeira/ Hammond B-3, Wade Jaynes/bass, and former Glass Harp drummer, John Sferra) provided plenty of instrumental fervor, too, which helped Keaggy's lyrics shine more brightly than they otherwise would have.

Most fans pointed to Keaggy's blistering Gibson Les Paul solos that finish off extended-play rockers such as "Stone Eyes" (7:01), "John the Revelator" (8:04), and "Doin' Nothin' " (8:25) as evidence that he finally got the magic on tape. True enough, but you can hear the abandon in Keaggy's voice as well. He cries, yelps, screams and lingers in falsetto-land on these tunes—and especially on the way-too-brief dark rocker, "Don't Pass Me By"—as though his life depended on it.

While we still await Keaggy's studio floodgates to completely open and drown us all, *Crimson and Blue* showed the world what he's capable of when given even a sliver of daylight to sparkle.

—*Dave Urbanski*

the songs

20 CRIMSON AND BLUE PHIL KEAGGY

SHOUTS OF JOY

WORLD OF MINE

EVERYWHERE I LOOK

LOVE DIVINE

REUNION OF FRIENDS

ALL THERE IS TO KNOW

WHEN WILL I EVER LEARN TO LIVE IN GOD

STONE EYES

I WILL BE THERE

DON'T PASS ME BY

JOHN THE REVELATOR

DOIN' NOTHIN'

NOTHING BUT THE BLOOD

twenty

twenty-on

Reunion 1986
Produced by John Potoker and Michael W. Smith

(21)

THE BIG PICTURE

MICHAEL W. SMITH

Michael W. Smith's first two albums, 1983's *Project* and 1984's *Michael W. Smith 2*, were, in retrospect, works in progress, documents that allowed the West Virginia native to work on the craft of recording while his fledgling record label Reunion Records got off the ground.

Reunion's co-owners/founders, Michael Blanton and Dan Harrell, were also serving another important function in Christian music: managing the hottest act in the business at the time, Amy Grant, whose *Unguarded* album the year before raised the bar for both musical invention and commercial success in this corner of the music industry.

Enter Smith—buoyed by new songwriting partner Wayne Kirkpatrick and sharing production duties with John Potoker (Genesis, Talking Heads, Brian Eno)—who took the proverbial ball and ran with it, radically changing his own sound while creating what may be his most consistently relevant album to date.

Where Smith's first two efforts were decidedly low-tech even by early '80s standards, *The Big Picture* opened the sonic floodgates. In the first

20 seconds of the album's opener, "Lamu," the listener gets buffeted by a pseudo-jet flying across the landscape, followed by a driving drum loop and scorching guitar that proved this record was absolutely nothing like what Smith had created in the past.

Blanton and Harrell put Kirkpatrick together with Smith after hearing a demo tape of some of the young Louisianan's songs. Kirkpatrick went on the road as a rhythm guitar player for Smith's first headlining tour after the *Michael W. Smith 2* record. It was on the road where their Elton John/Bernie Taupin-like songwriting relationship began, and *The Big Picture* was the first fruit of that collaboration.

The lyrical germ of *The Big Picture's* songs came from the letters Smith had received from young fans throughout the years, and if the creators had wanted to, a thread could have easily been drawn through the entire project, making it a rock opera/concept album along the lines of Styx's *Kilroy Was Here*. Thankfully, they resisted.

But the stories were there: tales of despair ("The Last Letter"), questions about sexual purity ("Old Enough to Know"), the pitfalls of apathy ("Goin' Thru the Motions") and the impact of pop culture and the media on a young person's moral development ("Wired for Sound"). Balancing those tough situations were the songs of hope ("Pursuit of the Dream"), encouragement ("You're Alright") and finding faith in the everyday paths of life ("Rocketown").

In a perfect world, *The Big Picture* would have been the album that launched Smith into superstardom, with production values that captured the ears of the general market merged with a message that appealed to fans already garnered in the Christian market. Instead, the reverse happened: pop radio paid no attention due to the subject matter, and Christian radio took a pass mostly because it was too darn loud.

But critics loved it, and *The Big Picture* set the table not only for Smith's future success two albums down the pike with *Go West Young Man*, but for the impact the team Smith's band (Kirkpatrick, guitarist Chris Rodriguez, bassist Chris Harris, keyboardist Mark Heimermann, drummer David Huff) would have on the face of Christian music in the years to come.

—*Lucas W. Hendrickson*

the songs

21 THE BIG PICTURE MICHAEL W. SMITH

LAMU

WIRED FOR SOUND

OLD ENOUGH TO KNOW

PURSUIT OF THE DREAM

ROCKETOWN

VOICES

THE LAST LETTER

GOIN' THRU THE MOTIONS

TEARIN' DOWN THE WALL

YOU'RE ALRIGHT

twenty-one

twenty-two

Essential 1995
Produced by Jars of Clay except for "Liquid" and
"Flood," produced by Adrian Belew

(22)

JARS OF CLAY

JARS OF CLAY

In a year when pop acts like Point of Grace, Amy Grant and Steven Curtis Chapman still dominated the charts, Jars of Clay came out of nowhere and stole the show. Was it an acoustic-based alternative band or a cleverly disguised folk act? Ultimately, it didn't matter—*Jars of Clay* was an immediate hit.

Formed in 1993 while its members were attending Greenville College in Illinois, Jars of Clay beat over 200 competitors in the Gospel Music Association's 1994 Spotlight talent contest, signaling the foursome's top spot as an unsigned act. It was a position the band wouldn't hold for long. On the heels of the group's win, Christian music label executives raced to snatch up copies of its independent release, *Frail*, and begin the fervent courting of the genre's latest and biggest buzz generator. By the summer of '94, the band had moved to Nashville, signed with Essential Records and entered the studio to work on its major label debut, a self-titled—and mostly self-produced—effort which released in May 1995 to critics' approval and fans' delight.

Opening the disc is "Liquid," an acoustic guitar and percussion odyssey that expertly weaves mandolin, violin and strings throughout an impassioned confession of "the one thing that I know... He didn't die for nothing." It's a strong signal of what was to come, an incredibly fresh journey through ten songs that speak directly to the faithful without using overtly religious language. Songs like "Love Song for a Savior" and "Like a Child" prayerfully plead for a more fervent relationship with God, but mostly the imaginative lyrics on *Jars of Clay* take a less overt route. The illusion of a facade-filled life takes front and center on "Boy on a String," a cut that creatively convicts the listener in its imagery of a puppet who only seeks to entertain. "Blind" focuses on someone who "can't find any reason to believe in love" while "He" addresses the atrocity of child abuse.

Musically, front man Dan Haseltine's voice—which grew stronger in later efforts—wrapped comfortably around inventive guitar parts courtesy of Steve Mason and Matt Odmark, while Charlie Lowell's subtle piano and organ arrangements provided support to each track. Strings and percussion from outside players gave the songs a just-perfect finishing touch.

Jars of Clay's star would continue to rise throughout the band's 1995 fall tour with PFR and the ensuing release of "Flood" to general market radio. Before long, Haseltine's eerily distorted vocal was rumbling "Rain, rain on my face" all across the nation's airwaves, transcending Jars of Clay into a household name as the video landed airplay on MTV and VH1. "Flood," which along with "Liquid" was produced by Adrian Belew (King Crimson, David Bowie), brought vast media attention, an opening slot for three Sting shows and sales in excess of two million copies.

Jars of Clay was a brilliant launch for this then college-aged foursome. Though its immense popularity would be attempted time and again, nothing has come close to matching this truly original and innovative album.

—*April Hefner*

the songs

22 JARS OF CLAY JARS OF CLAY

LIQUID
SINKING
LOVE SONG FOR A SAVIOR
LIKE A CHILD
ART IN ME
HE
BOY ON A STRING
FLOOD
WORLDS APART
BLIND
(HIDDEN TRACK)

twenty-th

Good News 1972
Producer: Love Song

(23)

LOVE SONG

LOVE SONG

At the height of its popularity, this pioneering foursome was referred to by many as "the Christian Beatles." It's not difficult to understand why. In the early '70s, when there wasn't much of a Christian music scene to speak of, the longhaired Southern California dudes in Love Song literally composed the rule book for a new kind of gospel music as they went along.

The baby band full of baby Christians took its first tentative steps through an open door at Chuck Smith's Calvary Chapel in 1970, playing acoustically and singing about the excitement of brand-new faith to a curious-but-welcoming crowd. By 1972, the group—Chuck Girard, a veteran of early '60s vocal groups The Castells ("Sacred") and The Hondells ("Little Honda") on keyboards, Tommy Coomes on guitar, Jay Truax on bass, and Bob Wall on guitar—had grown up spiritually and musically and finally made their first record, *Love Song*. Blending rock, folk, jazz and country sounds along with soaring, layered vocal harmonies that echoed the Beach Boys and Crosby, Stills & Nash, the Love Song sound was nothing short of revolutionary in the church. And with lyrics that spoke about

Christian faith in relevant, fresh ways, the *Love Song* album was an immediate hit among the radical young people of the "Jesus Movement."

In fact, Love Song helped bridge the chasm between the "old" and "new" church, between the hippies and the establishment. Their wild hair and clothes—juxtaposed with their gentle, humble spirits—said to skeptical onlookers that "the only thing that matters is commitment to Christ." It's a formula that Christian musicians of every stripe utilize to this day.

Despite the band's important contributions to Christian music, invoking the moniker "Love Song" today often elicits nostalgic smiles and "aww-weren't-those-folkies-cute" chuckles. That's unfortunate. There's real beauty and boldness on these 11 tracks that go way, way beyond the confines of simple folk music.

Of course the acoustic guitar is central to many songs, especially softer tunes like "Two Hands," "Welcome Back," and the opening ballad, "A Love Song," but this band rocked, too. The classic "Little Country Church"—recently covered on former Grammatrain front man Pete Stewart's solo debut—showcases exceedingly intricate, freewheeling electric guitar solos. "Freedom" begins innocently enough with soft piano and light drum passages, but the chorus unleashes a guitar-and-vocal combo that recalls John Lennon's harder-edged performances, also heard on the coda of "A Brand New

Song." Such musical elements aren't a big deal for Christian music in the new millennium, but they were radical and risky in 1972, and Love Song adapted its influences tastefully and adeptly. The band even employed the Phil Spector-esque production approach that shaped Girard's early career and chose to record the album at Spector's favorite Gold Star Studios where the legendary producer forged his '60s mini-symphonies.

With this groundbreaking recording—one that touched thematically on many issues close to the heart of a young, growing church—Love Song forever sealed its place as the Christopher Columbus of Christian music and discovered a brand new world.

—*Dave Urbanski*

the songs

(23) LOVE SONG   LOVE SONG

A LOVE SONG

CHANGES

TWO HANDS

LITTLE COUNTRY CHURCH

FREEDOM

WELCOME BACK

FRONT SEAT, BACK SEAT

LET US BE ONE

AND THE WIND WAS LOW

A BRAND NEW SONG

FEEL THE LOVE

A LOVE SONG (REPRISE)

Light 1976
Produced by Bill Maxwell & Andraé Crouch

(24)

THIS IS ANOTHER DAY

ANDRAÉ CROUCH
& THE DISCIPLES

Andraé Crouch is one of the most beloved of all modern Christian songwriters. Songs like "Through It All," "Bless His Holy Name," "I Don't Know Why (Jesus Loves Me)," "I've Got Confidence," "Jesus Is the Answer," "My Tribute" and literally dozens of others are bonafide classics. His songs have been recorded by everybody from Elvis to Pat Boone.

Crouch was 11 years old when his father, who was pastor of a small church, prayed that he would receive the gift of music. Almost immediately he began to play the piano and became the church pianist. In February of 1964, while in college, Andraé put a special group together he called "The Disciples," made up of twin sister Sandra (by then a successful studio percussionist) and vocalists Perry Morgan and Bili Thedford (who also played bass), and their reputation began to spread.

In 1969 Andraé met Ralph Carmichael, who urged him to record this new and exciting music God was giving him. An early single on Liberty Records called "Christian People" in 1970 earned the group their first Grammy nomination, but there would be many more where that came from. Carmichael signed the group to Light Records and released their first album, *Take the Message Everywhere*, in 1970.

This Is Another Day, coproduced by Andraé and drummer Bill Maxwell, was Crouch's seventh album, featuring a timely mix of contemporary gospel and '70s funk. As was his custom, Andraé shared lead vocals with various members of the Disciples—including Danniebelle Hall, James Felix, Perry Morgan and Sandra. The ten tracks feature top session players, including Joe Sample, Leon Russell, David Hungate, Dean Parks and Michael Brecker.

The album kicks off with the post-*Shaft,* pre-disco drive of "Perfect Peace," which segues into Danniebelle's soulful vocal on "My Peace I Leave with You." The group's jazz vocal arrangement of the title track gives way to the sublimely mellow "Quiet Times," followed by the album's most famous song, the majestic "Soon and Very Soon." The rest of the album continues in back-and-forth mode, alternating between beautiful praise songs like "We Expect You" or "All That I Have" and funky gems like "You Gave to Me" or "The Choice."

Seven albums were recorded during the group's 14-year tenure (before Andraé would begin a successful solo career in 1978), two of which would be honored with Dove Awards and two with Grammy Awards. His song "My Tribute (To God Be the Glory)," is now in the *Guinness Book of World Records* for being recorded over 3,000 times. Now in his 50s, Crouch is pastor of his late father's church and rarely records or performs.

In today's environment, Andraé Crouch may not stand out as much because there are so many quality artists, but in the mid-'70s this album stood head and shoulders above most contemporary releases. And it has stood the test of time, thanks to great songs, top-notch production and spirited performances.

—*John W. Styll*

the songs

(24) THIS IS ANOTHER DAY ANDRAÉ CROUCH & THE DISCIPLES

PERFECT PEACE/MY PEACE I LEAVE WITH YOU

THIS IS ANOTHER DAY

QUIET TIMES

SOON AND VERY SOON

WE EXPECT YOU

YOU GAVE TO ME

ALL THAT I HAVE

THE CHOICE

POLYNESIAN PRAISE SONG (I LOVE YOU)

twenty-four

twenty-fi

Fingerprint 1996
Compilation Producer: Dan Russell

25

ORPHANS OF GOD

VARIOUS ARTISTS

The music of Mark Heard rarely received much airplay and his albums never broke the six-figure sales mark, yet there've been few bigger influences on the evangelical rock intelligentsia. He was a deep thinker and cynic, whose sharp tongue on and off record didn't always endear him to labels and radio folks. But he also knew how to write a great pop hook like nobody's business, and toward the end of his career, Heard was belting out some of the most profoundly emotional, moving and unabashedly sentimental rock 'n' roll ever recorded. His work overflowed with love for nature and human relationships and, concurrently, an utter brokenness and insatiable hunger for heaven. You could give his records to your conservative Baptist cousin and radical atheist coworker and pretty much guarantee they'd both come back feeling he'd hit 'em where they lived.

Heard went on to the eternal reward he'd long ached for and sung about in 1992, after suffering two heart attacks, the first while onstage at the Cornerstone Festival. Both the grief over having lost such a unique voice and a thanksgiving for all the brilliant records Heard left behind was channeled into a pair of tribute albums: Myrrh's 1994 single-disc *Strong Hand of Love*, and two years later on

Fingerprint's *Orphans of God*, which reworked and expanded the previous release into a 34-track, two-CD set.

These were historic albums inasmuch as there had heretofore never been such an equal measure of acts who were alternately—to borrow the usual clichés—"Christian musicians" and "musicians who happen to be Christian." Certainly Bruce Cockburn had never shown up on the same collection as Rez Band's Glenn Kaiser; neither had lion Michael Been previously laid down with lamb Rich Mullins; nor had Victoria Williams and dc Talk's Kevin Smith been invited to the same party before.

Various epochs from Heard's long career were represented, from his late '70s day as an acoustic-strumming Larry Norman protege to his Byrds-ier recordings in the early '80s, to his multitracking one-man-band Ideola experiment of 1986, and finally and most satisfyingly, the rootsy but rockin' independent albums he released in the late '80s and early '90s. Phil Keaggy beautifully exemplified Heard's sweet side with "Everything Is Alright," while Tonio K. was just the curmudgeon for "Another Day in Limbo." Vigilantes of Love covered "Freight Train to Nowhere," and The Choir and Chagall Guevara made raucous sounds like a steam train to heaven, as if they might transport him the extra mile.

If there's anyone who's carried on in his spirit, it could be his friends Buddy and Julie Miller, who've subsequently won acclaim from the nation's top tastemakers, making "secular" music while being entirely upfront about their Christian principles. So it seems especially appropriate that they're the ones singing the title song, one of Heard's most affecting and restless anthems of the intrinsically alienated human condition, in memory of their pal who's orphaned no more.

—*Chris Willman*

ORPHANS OF GOD—BUDDY AND JULIE MILLER

WE KNOW TOO MUCH—MICHAEL BEEN

FREIGHT TRAIN TO NOWHERE—VIGILANTES OF LOVE

IT'S NOT YOUR FAULT—ASHLEY CLEVELAND

I JUST WANNA GET WARM—DAN RUSSELL

SATELLITE SKY—KATE TAYLOR

MERCY OF THE FLAME—PAT TERRY

RISE FROM THE RUINS—BROOKS WILLIAMS

STRONG HAND OF LOVE—BRUCE COCKBURN

WHAT KIND OF FRIEND—VICTORIA WILLIAMS

HOUSE OF BROKEN DREAMS—THE WILLIAMS BROTHERS

TIP OF MY TONGUE—TOM PRASADA-RAO

EVERYTHING IS ALRIGHT—PHIL KEAGGY

BIG AND STRONG—OLIVIA NEWTON-JOHN

ALL SHE WANTED WAS LOVE—BIG FAITH

ANOTHER GOOD LIE—HEZZE

TREASURE OF THE BROKEN LAND—CHAGALL GUEVARA

LONELY MOON—KEVIN SMITH

WORRY TOO MUCH—HARROD AND FUNCK

FIRE—BOB

BIG WHEELS ROLL—JOHN AUSTIN

RISE FROM THE RUINS—PARMIN SISTERS

WATCHING THE SHIPS GO DOWN—IAIN

ANOTHER DAY IN LIMBO—TONIO K.

LOVE IS SO BLIND—CAROLYN ARENDS

NOD OVER COFFEE—PIERCE PETTIS

REMARKS TO MR. MCLUHAN—RAMONA SILVER

LONG WAY DOWN—SWINGING STEAKS

LOOK OVER YOUR SHOULDER—RANDY STONEHILL AND KATE MINER

THREW IT AWAY—GLENN KAISER

DRY BONES DANCE—COLIN LINDEN

TIP OF MY TONGUE—THE CHOIR

STRONG HAND OF LOVE—DA

HAMMER AND NAILS—MARVIN ETZIONI

Sparrow 1990
Produced by Brown Bannister

26

SECRET OF TIME

CHARLIE PEACOCK

Charlie Peacock developed a legendary status in the '80s as a part of the Exit Records scene in Sacramento, California, and was responsible for launching Vector (of which he was an original member), The 77s and others. Early appearances at the Cornerstone Festival had earned him the reputation as the Christian equivalent to Sting. After an amazing but unsuccessful shot at the majors with his 1986 self-titled *Island* release, Peacock took to the indie scene, recording and releasing three volumes of his *West Coast Diaries* between 1987 and 1989. In 1990 Charlie did the unthinkable: he moved to Nashville and signed with Sparrow Records.

It was with great fear and trembling that fans approached his Sparrow debut, *The Secret of Time*. Though the difference a big budget could make was obvious right up front, Peacock had retained the artful adventurousness that had marked his independent career as well. A few songs from the West Coast releases were reprised, including the R&B-inflected "Big Man's Hat," which was a significant hit for the artist. Though the newer tunes like "Put the Love Back into Love" and "Dear Friend" came dangerously close to the AC line for some fans, gems like the atmospheric "Drowning Man" and the inspiring "One Thing" made up for it. On balance, *Secret of Time* is more of a lush pop record than anything resembling alternative or rock, but in 1990 the Christian scene didn't have a category for that kind of stuff, so Peacock got pegged as an alternative act anyway.

Secret of Time set the stage for Peacock's impressive discography in the '90s. The sonic perfection also earned him a reputation as an "A" level producer, something he would mine to great success in the coming years. With a range that spanned from upbeat dance tunes to deeply contemplative meditations, he had carved enough of a swath to keep things interesting for years to come.

—*John J. Thompson*

Atlantic 1991
Produced by Craig Krampf and Niko Bolas

27

BIG TOWN

ASHLEY CLEVELAND

Ashley Cleveland kicked around towns big (San Francisco) and not so big (Knoxville, Tennessee) before settling in Nashville in the mid-'80s. She quickly became a highly in-demand session singer, working with the likes of Steve Winwood, Patty Smythe and Emmylou Harris, and touring with John Hiatt's Goners in support of his *Slow Turning* album, on which she also sang.

Atlantic Records founder/chairman Ahmet Ertegun was impressed when he heard Cleveland's work on a Memphis Horns record, even more so when he heard her own compositions, and signed her to the label.

Big Town should have been 1991's feel-good story of the year. Here was a single mother, who by her own admission had given years of her life away to drugs and drinking, reclaiming her independence, asking the tough (yet at moments, hilarious) questions about relationships both physical and spiritual, all the while rocking your face off with her gutsy vocals.

Instead, *Big Town* was released to much critical acclaim and was easily that year's most Spirit-filled general market release, but was passed over by the tastemakers of the day. *Billboard* magazine called it one of that year's "ten most overlooked albums."

Christian music purists might dispute the claim that *Big Town* was a Christian album, choosing instead to claim Cleveland when she later signed with Reunion Records, for whom she recorded two highly regarded albums, one of which, *Lessons of Love,* earned Cleveland her first Grammy Award.

But after even one listen to the album's opener—the intro of Andraé Crouch's praise chorus "Soon and Very Soon" and the album's autobiographical title track—one can't help but walk away from *Big Town,* with its raw honesty, driving music and uncompromising statements of faith, with the feeling that any album Ashley Cleveland records is a "Christian album."

—*Lucas W. Hendrickson*

True North/Columbia 1980
Produced by Eugene Martynec

28

HUMANS

BRUCE COCKBURN

Canadian folk singer and poet Bruce Cockburn had won over Christian fans with early faith-statements in "Lord of the Starfields" and his testimony, "All the Diamonds." Following his American breakthrough *Dancing in the Dragon's Jaws* (number 42), Cockburn experienced a separation and divorce from his wife. Thus began an evolution in his music and theology that would move him beyond many Christian music fans' comfort zone.

While Cockburn had never had his head in the sand regarding life's difficulties, it was on *Humans* that he grappled with the problem of personal evil and the chaotic world most directly. The opening track,

"Grim Travellers," offered up one pilgrim's progress or the lack thereof, coming closer to a theology of exile in the culture. Cockburn's truth was a little closer to the bone of loss and doubt than most Christian artists ventured in those days (and even still).

In the face of his loss, Cockburn asked, "What about the bond/sealed in the loving presence of the Father?" while "Guerilla Betrayed," "How I Spent My Fall Vacation," "You Get Bigger As You Go" and "Tokyo" asked questions of ultimate purpose knowing that the simplistic answers of his young Christianity would not suffice. In "Fascist Architecture" he faced his own limitations and vowed new beginnings.

All was not loss. In "More Not More," Cockburn challenged what detracts from goodness, affirming "more songs, more warmth/more love, more life." Beneath the skin, he saw "Rumours of Glory," looking toward a resolution in God, "The Rose Above the Sky."

Cockburn would soon move away from folkier music, trying on rock, blues and new wave before returning to more familiar territory. Stark imagery, profanity, leftist political values and a more obscure expression of faith would challenge Christian fans, but Cockburn remains an artist who speaks truth with poetry and insight.

—*Brian Quincy Newcomb*

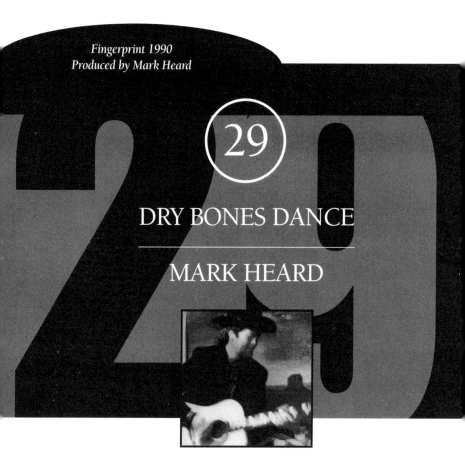

29

DRY BONES DANCE

MARK HEARD

Some would have seen it as just a pile of human remains, but Ezekiel saw it differently. The valley of dry bones in one of his visions was symbolic of the deadness of the human heart. There, in the midst of the decay, was the most powerful example of hope for him who had eyes to see.

Mark Heard was one of those rare poets who found God most intimately among the bones. He had refused the feel-good clichés so dominant in contemporary Christian music. After spending most of the '80s toiling in obscurity as an artist (see number 32, *Victims of the Age*), Heard had placed himself in a sort of exile, appearing under the pseudonymous moniker Ideola on the 1987 release *Tribal Opera* and as a producer, songwriter and engineer for other artists. In 1990 he joined with partners to form the Fingerprint label, and released his first solo record in over five years.

Dry Bones Dance emerged amidst the alternative revolution in rock and pop. Christian pop music was more placid and sweeter than ever, and the rock side was getting darker and heavier with each passing moment. In stark contrast to his ultra-hip Ideola project of 1987, *Dry Bones Dance* was a relaxed, acoustic, confident-sounding collection of country-folk-pop songs and ballads. The contributions of Sam Phillips, Pam Miner, Michael Been, Jerry Chamberlain, Sharon McCall and Fergus Marsh (among many others) brought a richness to Heard's wiry vocals and world-weary lyrics. The 14 songs all rank as classics, but particular standouts include the doggedly hopeful "Rise from the Ruins" and the sweet "Everything Is Alright."

Dry Bones Dance reinvigorated Heard's career and saw him enter a creative phase that rivaled any in his over 20-year stint. It became the unofficial "Part One" of a trilogy of albums that would eventually include the breathtaking *Second Hand* and the frenzied and exuberant *Satellite Sky*.

—John J. Thompson

A&M/Myrrh 1991
Produced by Brown Bannister,
Michael Omartian and Keith Thomas

30

HEART IN MOTION

AMY GRANT

Before it established her as one of A&M Records' most successful artists of all time, the era of Amy Grant's *Heart in Motion* began with a series of gasps within the community of Christian music fans.

(Gasp!) She's dancing with a man other than her husband in the video for "Baby, Baby"!

(Gasp!) She's using producers other than Brown Bannister for the first time in her career!!

(Gasp!) She doesn't use Jesus' or God's name in all of the songs!

In retrospect, every person, critic or fan alike, who expressed these sentiments either publicly or privately, needed to be told one thing: Relax.

Whatever her fans' fears, what *Heart in Motion* did was shine the light on her pop sensibilities and pull back the curtain on a creative community in Nashville that could be called upon to contribute more than just country music. It marked the first time a record out of Nashville's noncountry music community was recognized in the Grammy Awards' general categories, grabbing nominations for Best Pop Vocal Performance, Female and Best Pop Album.

Heart in Motion was a fun, upbeat pop record created by a young woman just entering her 30s who, knowing that she had been recording her own music for almost a decade and a half, wanted to spread her wings, gather in some new friends and collaborators, and see if the big, bad world of the general market would accept her. She did, and it did. Five million units worth and still counting—the bestselling album by a Christian music artist to date. End of story.

And to those detractors around at the time, admit it: you got a small thrill when you got in your car in that summer of '91 and heard the work of "one of our own," the omnipresent "Baby, Baby" dominating pop radio. You admit it? (Gasp!)

—*Lucas W. Hendrickson*

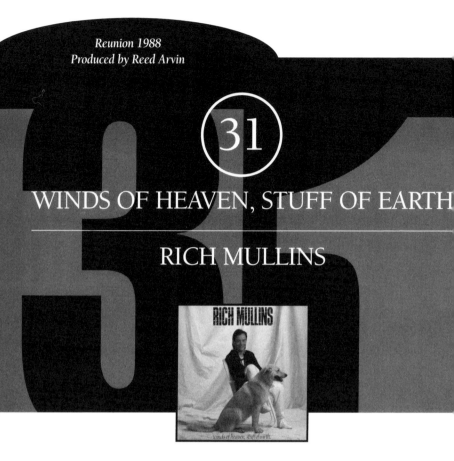

Within the image:

Reunion 1988
Produced by Reed Arvin

31

WINDS OF HEAVEN, STUFF OF EARTH

RICH MULLINS

It was no surprise when Mullins was posthumously awarded the 1999 Dove Award for Songwriter of the Year. Sure, he was a phenomenal musician, an engaging performer, a genuine yet unconventional artist through and through. But it was his lyrically vivid and earthy songs that captivated our souls.

Winds of Heaven, Stuff of Earth, Mullins' third album, boasts the song for which he will always be most closely associated, "Awesome God." His friends will tell you it was far from his favorite, but something about the power and passion of "Awesome God" struck a chord, resulting in its reign atop the country's Christian radio charts and its later inclusion in the hymnals of many sanctuaries in America. Backed by a 24-person choir, many of whom worked at his record label, the praise anthem does what Mullins did best—invites the listener to forget who's singing and be caught up in a worship experience of a grand, mysterious God.

But to define the Reed Arvin-produced *Winds of Heaven* by "Awesome God" alone would be missing so many great Mullins' moments: "The Other Side of the World," a call to missions recalling his own experiences overseas; "If I Stand," a heart-filled prayer to do all for the glory of God; "Such a Thing As Glory," an affirmation of the eternal home Mullins was so fond of imagining; and the "buzzes and beeps, shimmers and shines, rattles and patters and purrs" that filled the songwriter "With the Wonder" of creation, to name a few.

Winds of Heaven is not Mullins' musical masterpiece. But the recurrent themes of his life—his overwhelming need for God and his longing for heaven—whisper loudly time and again in this classic offering of songs, making it an essential recording for any collection.

—*April Hefner*

31

Home Sweet Home 1982
Produced by Mark Heard

32

VICTIMS OF THE AGE

MARK HEARD

Mark Heard had already proven himself as a gifted singer/songwriter with an impressive national debut on *Appalachian Melody* and *Stop the Dominoes* a year earlier, but it wasn't until the release of *Victims of the Age* that the full depth of his talent was apparent. In one of his best songs, later covered by Leslie Phillips, Heard was able to express the exile that envelops many modern Christians, and the sustaining reality of God's affectionate care:

"The world is in shambles/I'm just a young man but it's getting a little bit old to me/I'm already aching/The years have been taking a little bit of a toll on me/But way down in my heart of hearts/Way down in my soul of souls/I know that I am a fortunate man to have known Divine love" ("Heart of Hearts").

With street-wise poetry and worldly wise lyricism, Heard served up the sense of lostness and anonymity that defines modern urban life in the opening trilogy: the title track, "City Life Won't Let Up" and "Faces in Cabs." Faced with complexity, some bury their heads in the sand ("Growing Up Blind" and "Nothing Is Bothering Me"). Many Christians isolate themselves in cliques ("Dancing at the Policeman's Ball") or emphasize one issue to the exclusion of our call to compassion ("Everybody Loves a Holy War").

Heard invited a wider perspective and bolder expression of God's love. He knew that while many were living well, in "Some Folks' World" the situation was desperate and required a faithful response from followers of Jesus.

Featuring Heard's own fine guitar work and passionate vocals on music that moved from folk to Police/new wave rock, *Victims* insisted that Christians could and should engage the world we live in with honesty and hope rather than quiet desperation.

—*Brian Quincy Newcomb*

Sparrow 1992
Produced by Phil Naish

33

THE GREAT ADVENTURE

STEVEN CURTIS CHAPMAN

Like a motion picture soundtrack that serves as a catalyst to racing hearts, composer J. A. C. Redford's "Prologue" built and built to a crescendo that launched that ever-famous battle cry on the title track: "Saddle up your horses!"

After laboring for ten years as a songwriter and releasing four prior albums, *The Great Adventure* signaled the pinnacle of Steven Curtis Chapman's career to that point. And, surprisingly, it revealed an artist not content to settle for what had worked in the past. Instead, Christian music's boy-next-door took his number one charting title cut to heart and set out to blaze new musical trails.

The album reflects Chapman's acoustic singer/songwriter roots, though there's a decidedly pop sheen this time around. In fact, the Paducah, Kentucky, native stretches his wings with duet partners BeBe Winans (on "Still Called Today," a tender call to forgive) and dc Talk's Toby McKeehan (on the tongue-in-cheek "rap" parody with a point, "Got to B Tru"). "Where We Belong" and "That's Paradise" channel a heartland rock sound in the vein of John Mellencamp, with energetic electric guitar and a passionate vocal delivery.

But Chapman is most effective just being himself, a gifted communicator telling simple stories in simple ways. The unassuming acoustic guitar melody accented with low-key percussion on the pleading "Don't Let the Fire Die" works for a song of such intimacy. Piano and strings gently support "Heart's Cry," a personal testimony of Chapman's desire to be found faithful. And "Go There with You" follows on the heels of Chapman's beautiful and wedding-canonized ballad, "I Will Be Here" (from his third album, *More to This Life*), with a sweet and sappy reminder to his spouse of his commitment.

His first record to achieve gold status, *The Great Adventure* proved to be just that for Steven Curtis Chapman and the thousands of listeners who came along for the ride.

—*April Hefner*

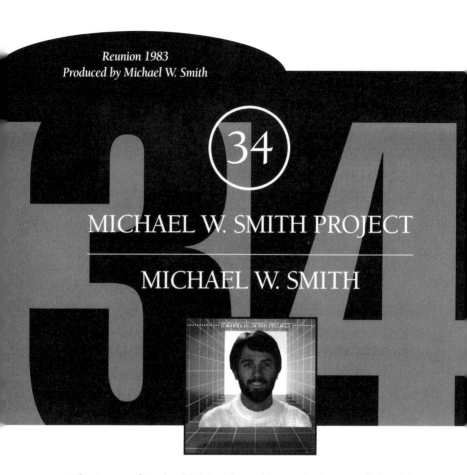

34

MICHAEL W. SMITH PROJECT

MICHAEL W. SMITH

The image of Michael W. Smith on (the original cover of) his debut album shows a conservatively clad, bearded West Virginia native whose smiling face brings to mind biblical figures rather than Hollywood hunks. Though years later this country boy with a penchant for piano playing would find himself on *People* magazine's "50 Most Beautiful People" list, *Project* was birthed back in the days before video had totally killed the radio star. All that mattered then was the music, and Smith certainly delivered.

Most notable, perhaps, for giving us that tear-jerking anthem sung at youth camps across the country—and the single most popular song in Christian music history—"Friends," *Project* also showcased Smith's talent for writing and arranging instrumentals with "Sonata in D Major," "Looking Up" and "Alpha Overture." Since then we've learned Smith's real musical passion is composing, as evidenced recently on his long-dreamed-of instrumental album.

Not that Smith has suffered for a lack of lyricists. Back before his fruitful songwriting partnership with Wayne Kirkpatrick, Smith's wife Debbie put words to his music. In fact, Michael W. Smith's better half is credited with all the lyrics here, including "Great Is the Lord," which struck such a chord with the church that it's since been immortalized in many modern hymnals. "Could He Be the Messiah" and "Be Strong and Courageous" also showcased Smith's more worshipful side, while "The Race Is On" and "You Need a Saviour," seem, in retrospect, to be precursors to *The Big Picture* and *I 2 Eye*.

In just a few short years Smith's career would take a decided turn toward the teen market. Those changes left some fans longing for another project like *Project*, but whatever Smith does in the future, it only serves to make this debut seem even more full of promise.

—*Wendy Lee Nentwig*

Word 1995
Produced by Brown Bannister

35

MY UTMOST FOR HIS HIGHEST

VARIOUS ARTISTS

The brainchild of Word Records' executive Loren Balman, *My Utmost for His Highest* was a make-or-break experiment. Based on the collection of Scottish preacher Oswald Chambers' writings by the same title, the album was a big budget, big name, big risk event—a completely original various artists' collection unlike anything Christian music had seen before.

Strings by the London Session Orchestra adorn eight of the 11 songs with a beauty and depth much more common to classical music than pop. But Nashville's leading session players—along with top song-writers like Michael W. Smith, Wayne Kirkpatrick, Cindy Morgan,

Amy Grant, Twila Paris and Steven Curtis Chapman—keep the project accessible to any crowd.

4HIM's harmonies never sounded tighter than on "You Are Holy," and producer Brown Bannister's Midas touch brings new depth and character to the vocals of Chapman ("Sometimes He Comes in the Clouds") and Point of Grace ("Hold On to Me").

Lyrically, *My Utmost* is straightforward praise and worship, a celebration of and call to the relationship between the Creator and the created. In one of the album's most moving moments, Gary Chapman recalls the emotion and zeal of Psalmist David in "Man After Your Own Heart," a song written by Kirkpatrick and Billy Sprague. Cindy Morgan confidently wails on her self-penned "You'll Be There," as Bryan Duncan wonders how such a perfect God could love "A Heart Like Mine." And Grant's "Lover of My Soul" rejoices in the notion that "the Maker of this whole wide world is a Father to me."

A trendsetter for its time, many such multiartist compilations have since attempted to achieve the excellence (and sales) of *My Utmost for His Highest*, including a sequel project in the *My Utmost* line. But the original stands alone in its reach for superlative quality.

—*April Hefner*

36

MEDALS

RUSS TAFF

One would be hard pressed to find another artist, in this or any other musical genre, who has reinvented themselves as many times as Russ Taff.

Medals, Taff's second solo effort, falls squarely between the "former lead singer of the Imperials" vibe found on his solo debut *Walls of Glass* and the troubled, introspective nature of his 1987 self-titled project.

Certainly, with its mid-'80s SoCal pop sheen, *Medals*' emphasis is on the production and the songs. Coproduced by Taff and Jack Joseph

Puig (who got his start engineering for Brown Bannister on Amy Grant albums and later went on to pop success in the '90s, producing tracks for bands like Tonic, Jellyfish and Semisonic), *Medals* set the artistic standards of its time.

On the musical side, top-notch players such as Paul Leim and Lenny Castro (drums/percussion), Dann Huff and Michael Landau (guitars), Nathan East and Neil Stubenhaus (bass), and singers Tommy Funderburk, Bill Champlin and Tata Vega all contributed greatly. Russ and his wife, Tori, wrote or cowrote eight of the album's ten songs, with contributions from Chris Eaton, James Newton Howard, Roby Duke and Pam Mark Hall.

But the historical value of *Medals* comes in the shape of having something of this quality available to the public at a time when Christian music was just starting to make headway in the mainstream. Amy Grant's *Unguarded* was just beginning to blow up, and the genre needed a male counterpart at which it could point and say, "Look over here! Christian pop music isn't just about Amy!"

Medals served that purpose, and while Taff would never go on to achieve the success of a Michael W. Smith or a Steven Curtis Chapman, this album was his most commercially rewarded. More importantly, Russ Taff is one of Christian music's most distinctive— and imitated—vocalists and *Medals* showcased his talents beautifully.

—*Lucas W. Hendrickson*

Sparrow/Capitol 1988
Produced by Keith Thomas

37

HEAVEN

BEBE & CECE WINANS

For much of the '80s, BeBe & CeCe Winans had been about the work of expanding the parameters of contemporary soul gospel into the glossiest of adult R&B terrain. The siblings' first gospel radio hit came with a reworking of the pop hit, "Up Where We Belong," back when they were still affiliated with The PTL Club.

The duo's subsequent debut for Sparrow/Capitol yielded them some mainstream adult contemporary and R&B play with "I.O.U. Me." *Heaven* broke the duo through to true star status with an even more stylized sound. BeBe's lyrics likewise succeeded at being interpreted as specifically Christian in their devotion or more spiritually ecumenical for all-purpose inspiration.

Calculated as it all might have appeared, it made for some catchy and creative Christian music. "Heaven," the collection's biggest R&B hit, shone with regality and a compelling, complex melody. Just as that number was buoyed by an insistent groove, "Celebrate New Life" gave the Winans' another dance floor anthem. "Hold Up the Light" took a similar melody and wed it to sentiments in tune with the Reagan/Bush era's spirit of volunteerism and "Just Say No" sentiments. The presence of Whitney Houston on the song elicited a "hey!" from the crossover contingent even as it garnered a "huh?" from stauncher gospel patrons.

Voices as nuanced and lustrous as BeBe's & CeCe's positively glow on slow jams, a quantity not lacking on *Heaven*. Back-to-back solo turns for BeBe and CeCe on "Meantime" and "Don't Cry," followed a little later with a walloping rendition of Simon & Garfunkel's "Bridge Over Troubled Waters," provides a righteous summation of the twosome's balladic power.

These young Winans took flak from many for making sanctified R&B with such an upwardly mobile sound. *Heaven* nevertheless remains a landmark in the dialogue between gospel and R&B and brings together a shared audience for both.

—*Jamie Lee Rake*

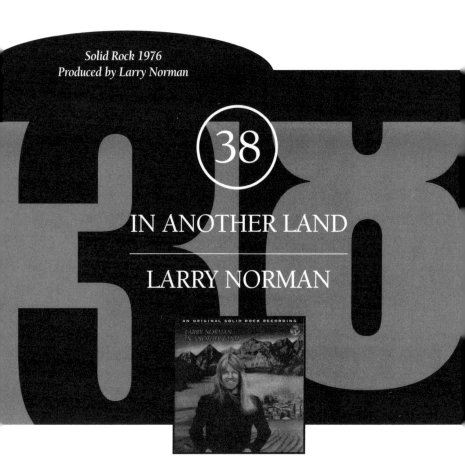

Solid Rock 1976
Produced by Larry Norman

(38)

IN ANOTHER LAND

LARRY NORMAN

38

IN ANOTHER LAND

LARRY NORMAN

"I've searched all around the world to find a grain of truth/I've opened the mouth of love and found a wisdom tooth." With fresh cultural awareness and great lines like that, Larry Norman was a true pioneer, taking the simple gospel message of Jesus Christ and applying his considerable talents to creating pop rock that would speak to fans of the Beatles, Stones and Bob Dylan. With his best work starting out on mainstream labels and underground recordings, Solid Rock Records was Norman's company, an effort to get his own music out in more conventional Christian circles and give support to newcomers like Randy Stonehill, Mark Heard and Tom Howard.

About half of *In Another Land* had appeared on the rare basement recordings, *Street Level* and *Bootleg*. Classic Norman songs like "I Love You," "U.F.O.," "Righteous Rocker," "Six Sixty Six," "One Way" and "Song for a Small Circle of Friends" had become concert mainstays, and they were offered here for the first time in state-of-the-studio recordings. This core provided the heart of this new recording, which introduced "The Rock That Doesn't Roll," an appropriately rockin' song that featured the high-voiced Norman in one of his grittiest vocal performances.

In addition, "Shot Down" responded humorously to numerous rumors that Norman had fallen away from the fold, and "I Am a Servant" put the early Christian rocker's faith witness into a ballad form that gained him his first significant Christian radio airplay. Norman not only broke the ground that allowed Christian rock 'n' roll to grow, he provided the arguments and witness that made it tenable to many.

Norman would never again match the power and quality of the songs delivered here, supported by Randy Stonehill on second guitar and harmony vocals, but there's little argument against the monumental contribution he made to this youthful genre.

—*Brian Quincy Newcomb*

Gospo Centric 1998
Produced by Kirk Franklin

39

THE NU NATION PROJECT

KIRK FRANKLIN

KIRK FRANKLIN

THE NU NATION PROJECT

He's not much of a singer, but that ain't no big thang to Kirk Franklin, the undisputed leader of contemporary gospel music—and its biggest risk taker. Why risk taker? In addition to his eyebrow-raising, dance-oriented concerts, Franklin's friendships and collaborations with the likes of Salt 'N' Pepa, Usher and R. Kelly have attracted a ton of controversy.

Undeterred by the too-worldly-for-Christians, too-Christian-for the-world grumbling, Franklin produced and cowrote 1997's *God's Property* album (featuring the hit single "Stomp") which went double platinum and earned Franklin a Grammy for Producer of the Year.

But that was just the beginning. Franklin's *The Nu Nation Project*, released the next year, broke down racial, musical and religious barriers like nothing else before it. The album's centerpiece—a rousing ballad called "Lean on Me" featuring Kelly, Crystal Lewis, Mary J. Blige and even U2's Bono—captured the essence of Franklin's mission: To reach blacks and whites, hip-hoppers and rockers, and people within and without the church.

Indeed, kickin' tracks like the opening "Revolution"—cowritten by Franklin and super-producer Rodney Jerkins—are interspersed with gentle, inspired ballads like "Something About the Name Jesus," "Hold Me Now" and "He Loves Me." And gospel-tinged tunes such as "Riverside," "Smile Again" and "If You've Been Delivered" don't allow you to forget where Franklin's musical roots are. There's no shortage of humor, either. "Interlude: The Car (Stomp)" answers Franklin's critics via an older, hilarious, Reverend James Cleveland-loving couple who bow to Franklin's feet then diss him behind his back.

With *The Nu Nation Project*, Franklin definitely attracted more naysayers. But it didn't matter—it also attracted an even bigger audience of God-praising listeners of every age, color and denomination.

Just the right recipe for a nu nation, huh?

—*Dave Urbanski*

Myrrh 1983
Produced by Brown Bannister

40

A CHRISTMAS ALBUM

AMY GRANT

Coming off the bar-raising success of *Age to Age,* Amy Grant was ready for a slight diversion before showing her next artistic hand, a move she used later with a second holiday album after *Heart in Motion.* Amy went back to Jim Guercio's Caribou Ranch in Colorado for the second in what would be four albums she would record there. During the summer of 1983, she and her team crafted a contemporary Christmas classic that would reach beyond the walls of the subculture like none before it.

With a savvy combination of traditional carols, modern-era standards and five original songs for the season, *A Christmas Album* was not only well received by her fans (providing the industry with its first gold-selling Christmas record), but came to be purchased and loved by thousands in the mainstream market.

Though not the first Christmas album released in the Christian pop music world (that would be 1977's *Come On Ring Those Bells* by Evie), *A Christmas Album* gave the world songs that took on a life of their own. "Tennessee Christmas," written by Grant and Gary Chapman, has been recorded and performed more times than anyone can count by both pop and country artists. Michael W. Smith's "Emmanuel" received immediate pop radio airplay the year it released, was later recorded by Smith himself and featured on a myriad of Christmas tours, including Grant's. It, along with "Christmas Hymn" (cowritten by Smith and Grant), was also performed for the President on the annual *Christmas in Washington* concert telecast on NBC, and resides in many modern hymnals today.

Perhaps it was the one time of year when pop culture was open to listening to the work of contemporary Christian artists, but whatever the reason, *A Christmas Album* became the number one selling holiday album for years in the pop market—a feat Amy would repeat again in 1992 with *Home for Christmas*.

—*Thom Granger*

Island 1981
Produced by Steve Lillywhite

41

OCTOBER

U2

The Irish quartet's sophomore effort is marked by two significant, clashing catalysts: the newfound Christian faith of singer Bono, guitarist the Edge and drummer Larry Mullen Jr.; and the backstage theft of a briefcase containing all of Bono's lyric ideas just weeks before recording was to commence.

So with the band under the gun and Bono literally composing words at the studio mike, *October* became U2's broken-play project—a record fueled by equal measures of spiritual passion and deadline desperation.

Bono's heartfelt Christian conviction bleeds all over the very first track, "Gloria." Here the 20-year-old vocalist intones the frenetic song's (mostly) Latin chorus, and you know he believes what he's singing: "Gloria in te domine/Gloria exultate/Gloria, Gloria/Oh Lord, loosen my lips..."

Similar themes are evident all over *October*. The icy, piano-drenched title track—which became a well-known live prelude to *War*'s "New Year's Day"—speaks of humanity's transitory nature and God's eternal nature. "Fire" explores apocalyptic imagery, "With a Shout" focuses on the Jerusalem hill where Christ died and "Scarlet" is the album's simplest tune, an atmospheric piece in which Bono simply repeats one word, "rejoice." And the Gaelic, uilleann pipe-driven "Tomorrow" features Bono's most explicit Christian lyrics ever: "Open up to the Lamb of God/To the love of He who made the blind to see/He's coming back...I believe it."

Such statements certainly were not *de rigueur* for rock bands in 1981, especially for the college-age, postpunk army that U2 had been marching in. Neither was this album's sound, defined by Gregorian chants and the Edge's ringing, ethereal guitars instead of quirky new wave styles. Yet this patchwork creation shook awake the souls of countless music fans, increased U2's popularity and made singing about faith downright cool. What's more, *October* made U2 the "alternative to alternative": a musical and spiritual statement that put the group in a camp by itself.

—*Dave Urbanski*

True North/Millennium 1979
Produced by Eugene Martynec

(42)

DANCING IN THE DRAGON'S JAWS

BRUCE COCKBURN

The quiet epiphany evident in the lyrics of Bruce Cockburn's 1974 *Salt, Sun & Time* began a period where the Canadian singer/songwriter illuminated a more clearly Christian theological point of view in his poetic lyrics. 1978's *Further Adventures Of* captured the imagination of *CCM* magazine's editors enough for them to publish a glowing review, but it was *Dancing in the Dragon's Jaws* that brought Cockburn not only his biggest hit single in the U.S., but acceptance (and distribution) in the Christian market.

Part of that was due to the hit single, "Wondering Where the Lions Are." A reflection of spiritual peace and joy that could rival the 23rd

Psalm, "Lions" was a bouncy, upbeat tune that boldly declared:

"You be in me and I'll be in you/Together in eternity/Some kind of ecstasy got a hold on me/And I'm wondering where the lions are…"

The song was a big enough hit to land him a guest spot on *Saturday Night Live* in 1979, and it caught the attention of Word Records executives enough to license the album for Christian bookstore distribution on its Myrrh label.

Despite the fact that most of *Dragon's Jaws'* lyrics made heavier use of poetry and metaphor than most Christian music of the time (or this time, for that matter), there was enough specificity in lines like, "You can take the wisdom of this world/And give it to the ones who think it all ends here" and "So love the Lord and in Him love me too/And in Him go your way and I'll be right there with you/Leaving no footprints when we go" to gain the trust of the Christian music enthusiast.

It was never to be the case again. Though Cockburn has continued to create literate, thoughtful and spiritual music, the lack of specific biblical language and the presence of the occasional political agenda and four-letter word has kept his recordings out of the Christian market.

—*Thom Granger*

Word 1996
Produced by Michael Omartian, Phil Naish,
Scott Williamson and Blair Masters

43

LIFE, LOVE AND OTHER MYSTERIES

POINT OF GRACE

When Terry Jones, Shelley Breen, Heather Lewis and Denise Jones first appeared in Christian music in 1993, no one could have predicted the impact the four Ouachita Baptist University alums would have as Point of Grace. At the time of this book's publication, that impact includes one platinum and three gold albums, eight Dove Awards, media impressions too numerous to recount and 21 consecutive number one songs—all with simple four-part harmonies and direct-to-the-youth-group pop songs.

But the numbers aren't really what this quartet is about. Their mission is to share songs of life, love and the mysteries of God with the cavalcade of young women for whom they hope to be role models. And that's exactly what they did on *Life, Love and Other Mysteries*, the group's third album.

Setting the thematic agenda, the four women pulled in some of Christian music's leading talents to write the album. Regie Hamm, Jeff & Gayla Borders, Scott Krippayne, Michael Omartian, Kyle Matthews and others provided the lyrically inspirational direction Point of Grace demanded. Omartian and the other producers brought a sonic fullness and vocal strength far beyond previous efforts. Musically, the album stepped in adventurous directions with more inventive harmony arrangements, jazzier melodies and more confidently delivered vocal leads.

Song highlights include "Keep the Candle Burning," an up-tempo anthem of encouragement to all those experiencing dark nights, and "Circle of Friends," an acoustically pleasing tune celebrating relationships near and far. Perhaps the riskiest and most moving cut—the piano-based ballad "God Forbid" in which Lewis ably displays subtle vocal nuances as well as her tremendous range—cautions the familiarity with which Christians all-too-often approach their Creator.

All in all, *Life, Love and Other Mysteries* finds the members of Point of Grace growing as women and artists, pushing the envelope in appropriate places while honing the skills and message for which they had become known.

—*April Hefner*

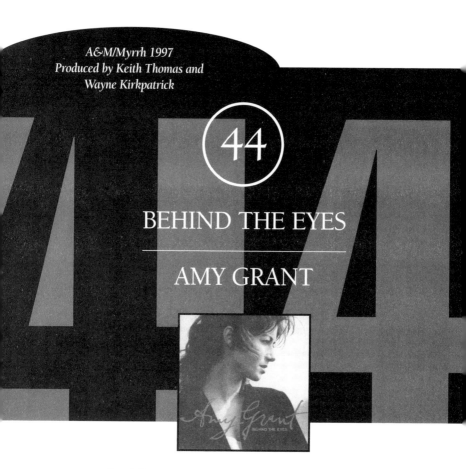

A&M/Myrrh 1997
Produced by Keith Thomas and
Wayne Kirkpatrick

44

BEHIND THE EYES

AMY GRANT

It must be difficult being synonymous with an entire movement. Amy Grant was just that. Mention Christian music to the average person on the street and 90 percent of the responses would involve her. She had become such a dominating figure that there were literally miles between her and whoever was coming in second in any given month. The dark side of that kind of pressure began to show its head when Grant wrote and recorded her 1997 magnum opus *Behind the Eyes*.

The warmth of tone, acoustic instrumentation and a more low-key vocal approach were welcomed improvements over the sometimes-stale synthetics on *House of Love* and the overly youthful sound of *Heart in Motion*. On *Behind the Eyes*, Grant was acting her age and bringing her over 20 years of experience to bear in a way that was new to her and her fans.

Her 1988 album *Lead Me On* had explored similar lyrical themes and musical shades, but unlike the former, *Eyes* was a largely self-penned effort. The reflective tone seemed to glide over a stream of melancholy. "Nobody Home" told the story of an economic turnaround that destroyed a small town, but seemed to be about something more. Maybe the small town was a metaphor for her family? In fact, most of the songs seemed to speak on at least two levels. On one hand there was the literal interpretation of the lyrics themselves. On the other there were poetic inferences that seemed to be more about her personal struggles. Regardless of the actual intent, to hear this kind of artistry coming from the figurehead of a genre not usually known for honest soul-searching was an encouragement in and of itself.

—John J. Thompson

Reunion 1992
Produced by Mark Heimermann and
Michael W. Smith

45

CHANGE YOUR WORLD

MICHAEL W. SMITH

Michael W. Smith had already changed his world considerably when his eighth and biggest-selling album, *Change Your World*, hit the shelves in August of 1992. A mainstream distribution deal with Geffen not only took his previous studio recording *Go West Young Man* to the general market masses, it also rewarded this native West Virginian with an American Music Award.

While Smith later admitted that he fought to keep his head on straight during that season of unprecedented success, *Change Your World* reveals a Christian worldview that remained fully intact despite the undertow that often accompanies fame and fortune.

Aside from the outspoken "Cross of Gold," there are few overt references to his Christian faith on this recording; however, if one considers marital faithfulness, racial reconciliation, committed friendship, inner beauty and sacrificial love important Christian virtues, Smith hit the proverbial nail on the head. Two singles rocketed to the top of the pop charts: "I Will Be Here For You" (cowritten with Grammy-winning songwriting sensation Diane Warren) and "Somebody Love Me," while "Give It Away" and the album's opener, "Picture Perfect," held the number one spot on several Christian radio charts simultaneously.

Musically, many have said that *Change Your World* is the perfect hybrid between the edgy, harder sound of *The Big Picture* and the pop element so prevalent on his more commercially successful recordings. Smith coproduced the album with Mark Heimermann, a collaboration that wrapped outstanding hooks in a smooth yet often intense pop vibe. Also included on the disc is a duet with Amy Grant ("Somewhere, Somehow") and an updated version of the classic, "Friends." While Smith has since made several highly acclaimed and successful recordings, due to the unique musical blend, the weighty songwriting and the immense pop success of *Change Your World*, it remains for many the definitive Michael W. Smith record.

—*Laura Harris*

46

IMMIGRANT'S DAUGHTER

MARGARET BECKER

From her stint in the late-'80s as a pioneering rock chick to her multifaceted pop reincarnations in the '90s, Margaret Becker has never been afraid to test the boundaries of Christian music. Call her Lilith Fair material, only about a decade ahead of her time.

On *Immigrant's Daughter*, her third effort, Becker writes in the liner notes that these songs deal with "a human plea for holiness and righteousness and a godly answer of mercy and grace." What she doesn't tell us is that this is an album that is both worship and prayer, proclamation and plea. Not to mention that it's exceptionally well done, thanks in part to her commanding presence on acoustic guitar (as well as that of Jimmy Abegg, who contributed both acoustic and electric parts). And for the first time with Becker, Charlie Peacock takes the producer reins and with fine results, so fine that he helmed her next three projects.

But what sets Becker apart from the masses on this, and all her records, is that voice. All guts and grit one minute, then immaculately pristine in the next phrase, her voice is unpredictable, ardent and forceful. In a word: amazing. You don't simply want to listen, you *have* to listen.

A natural storyteller, Becker opens her personal journal on *Immigrant's Daughter* and pours forth songs of her heritage, her passions, her desire for a deeper faith and her vision of the future. The title cut honors "the simple faith, the silent strength" of her grandmother while "This Is My Passion" and "The Hunger Stays" convincingly illustrate her need for God. The typically serious songwriter indulges her Irish whimsy on the almost irritatingly perky "Solomon's Shoes" and the encouraging "Laugh a Little." But it's on the vulnerable and tender ballad, "Just Come In," spoken from God's perspective, in which Becker's gifts shine the brightest, revealing with incomparable beauty the grace of a Redeemer who welcomes prodigals home.

—*April Hefner*

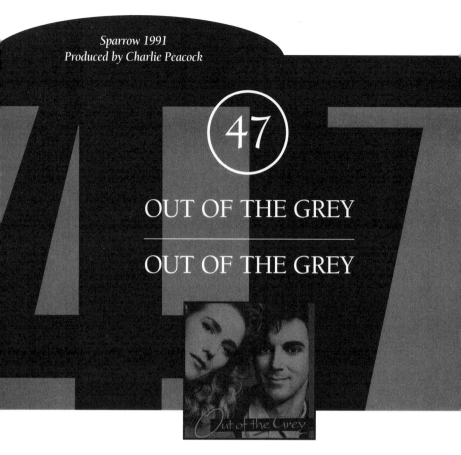

Sparrow 1991
Produced by Charlie Peacock

47

OUT OF THE GREY

OUT OF THE GREY

In a live setting, which is still perhaps the ultimate way to hear Out of the Grey, she's the straight answer to his sarcastic witticisms, the moments of vocal purity and beauty to offset his possessed and passionate displays on the acoustic guitar. In the early '90s, audiences were first treated to a taste of this relationship set to music when the duo of Scott and Christine Denté introduced a brand of pop that could be both alternative and accessible. The dance had begun.

Meeting in 1985 at the Berklee College of Music in Boston, the couple married in 1987 and moved to Nashville the following year where they recorded demos whenever they weren't waiting tables.

Eventually, the twosome caught the ear of Sparrow Records' Peter York and entered the studio with Charlie Peacock in the producer's chair.

Christine's voice—often ethereal and breathy but never weak—immediately captured attention, causing one reviewer to deem it "one of the most perfectly tuned instruments in Christian music." Meanwhile, Scott's biting and inventive turns on electric and acoustic guitars were balanced against Peacock's clean, simple production, which let the songs speak for themselves.

Ah, yes, the songs. Artful and intelligent, *Out of the Grey* offers relevant expressions of life and faith, of longing and discovery, of wonder and certainty, all basked in a light of faith that is apparent without being preachy. In fact, many of the songs recall the struggle to acknowledge Christ in the first place, an experience the couple knew well as Christine had shared the gospel with her then-unbelieving friend Scott during their college years. Album opener "Wishes" reveals the desire to see a loved one "on the other side of heaven's door," while closer "The Deep" asks, "Can you hear the deep/Calling you to sea/It's a siren song of peace." In between are eight tunes—including trademark OOTG cuts "He Is Not Silent" and "Remember This"—that are still relevant, still moving and still the best representation of Out of the Grey's indisputable talent.

—*April Hefner*

Light 1984
Produced by Bill Maxwell and Scott V. Smith

(48)

TOMORROW

THE WINANS

One of the key building blocks in the foundation of contemporary soul gospel is the second album by The Winans. The first group of the sibling dynasty to record, these four brothers—Marvin, Carvin, Michael and Ronald—made one album for Ralph Carmichael's Light Records before *Tomorrow*, but this one represented the foursome's early artistic peak.

Produced by former Andraé Crouch & the Disciples drummer Bill Maxwell and Scott V. Smith, *Tomorrow* featured songs with arrangements that built logically on Crouch's '70s work. The tracks were played by Andraé's core musicians—Harlan Rogers, Hadley

Hockensmith, Justo Almario, Alex Acuña and the aforementioned Maxwell—who would become known in L.A. jazz circles as Koinonia, and go on to influence the development of a new sound in contemporary jazz on the West Coast. Their influence gave *Tomorrow* a sound that had much more in common with the post-disco R&B of the early '80s (pre-Quincy Jones-era Michael Jackson) than it did with the "contemporary" gospel of the day. The album's slick, sophisticated grooves were replete with enough touches of mellow string and horn arrangements to go down easy with the kind of audiences that embraced groups like Earth, Wind & Fire.

Moreover, the album showed all four brothers to be a storehouse of talent. They penned all of the album's ten songs, and all of them took turns at lead vocals that made one wish for a crossover hit. No such luck—especially disappointing in the case of the title tune and "Bring Back the Days of Yay and Nay," the album's best songs. It was one of those moments when fans knew they were hearing a best-kept secret...and wanted desperately to tell it to the world. This time around, it was not to be—but there would be plenty of that for the whole family later on.

—*Thom Granger*

Pretty Good Records 1980
Produced by Bill Maxwell and Keith Green

49

SO YOU WANNA GO BACK TO EGYPT

KEITH GREEN

This truly unique album was wrought in the midst of radical changes in Green's music ministry and his spiritual life. One big external change came a few months before recording began, when his "Last Days" community—his wife Melody, kids and a few dozen down-and-out young people who lived with them—packed up their long-time, posthippie, Los Angeles-based household and moved to Lindale, Texas, where Last Days thrived for years afterward.

On deeper levels, the revival-like experiences during performances at Oral Roberts University the year before profoundly refocused Green's approach to music ministry—the emphasis increasingly going to *ministry*. Besides giving free concerts, one way he put this vision into action was by convincing Billy Ray Hearn to let him out of his freshly signed Sparrow contract so he could offer his forthcoming album for "whatever you can afford." It was a radical move that affronted the entire Christian music business, and all the more radical 20 years later as Christian music reaches unprecedented levels of commercial power.

All these changes—not to mention learning the meaning of God's grace the hard way—influenced the still-fresh tone of *So You Wanna Go Back to Egypt*. While Green acknowledges in the liner notes that "this album may seem a bit sad at times," there's plenty of interwoven joy—even humor—in the grooves. The title track, even with its serious message, is hilarious. And that's part of what makes this record unique. Other songs with weighty themes are backed with peppy music ("Unless the Lord Builds the House," "You Love the World (And You're Avoiding Me)," "Lies"), and they make for a more holistic emotional experience. The album also contains the worship classic "Oh Lord You're Beautiful" and a harmonica solo from a newly converted Bob Dylan on "I Pledge My Head to Heaven."

—*Dave Urbanski*

Myrrh 1988
Produced by Derri Daugherty and
Steve Hindalong with Gene Eugene
and Steve Griffith

50

CHASE THE KANGAROO

THE CHOIR

Growing out of the '80s Christian alt/rock explosion in Southern California, The Choir had learned from Daniel Amos and forged a truly original sound. In Derri Daugherty's chiming guitars paired with Steve Hindalong's driving human rhythms on drums, and deeply personal and often humorous, metaphorical lyrics of a faith lived out in the present tense, The Choir had discovered a unique artistic voice.

Backed by bassist Tim Chandler and Buckeye Dan Michaels on sax and lyricon, Hindalong and Daugherty dug deep to create a bold statement. Strong, melodic rock compositions engaged the listener, but it was the passion in the lyrics and Daugherty's vocal delivery—together with the overall energy of the instrumental arrangements—that lifted this album above the norm. The challenge to be true artists while seeking God's direction and maintaining day jobs surfaces in the playful title track. "Shovel go deep, heart be true," was a prayer for integrity.

Guided by keen philosophical insights, "Consider," "Children of Time" and "Clouds" were edgy power pop that engaged the mind and trusted the listener to figure out what was what. That quality and a visceral musicality marked The Choir as one band Christians could share with their nonbelieving friends. Though quirky, "The Rifleman" and "Everybody in the Band" revealed their twisted humor while making serious statements.

The courage to speak the truth in love informed the difficult emotions of "Sad Face." At a time when most Christian music tended toward a "Don't Worry, Be Happy" understanding of life in Christ, Hindalong wrote about the sad experience of his wife's miscarriage. He found encouragement to be honest about the pain and hardship in Ecclesiastes 7:3: "Sorrow is better than laughter, because a sad face is good for the heart."

Art that sprang from real life, a Christian band that rocked with intensity, The Choir was the real deal.

—*Brian Quincy Newcomb*

PMG 1998
Produced by Victor and Cedric Caldwell,
Keith Crouch, Lauryn Hill, Victor Massando,
Tony Rich, Tommy Sims, Darryl Simmons,
Chak Daddy, Babyboy
and E. Dawk

51

EVERLASTING LOVE

CECE WINANS

cece
winans

everlasting love

CeCe Winans has made weighty contributions to contemporary gospel's growth. If you have ever seen the lady in concert, however, you might get the impression that she missed her calling.

Everlasting Love gave CeCe Winans a platform for taking her message to the lost and hopeless as well as those who let themselves get lost after once having known the narrow way. In her co-executive producer capacity, Winans allowed herself access to fresh songwriting and studio talent that aided her in making a consummate 13-song slice of adult R&B.

Keith Crouch (Andraé's nephew) gave a jolt of groove juice to the first single and biggest radio hit, "Well, Alright." Crouch worked with appropriately grander strokes when Winans took on God's narrative voice for "I Am."

Winans broached jazzier terrain on "Slippin'," where a chunky, molasses-slow rhythm complements a warning to a backslider. More celebratory, though equally creative, is the South African choral accompaniment to "Feel the Spirit."

"What About You" found producer Tony Rich shining up the languid acoustic soul texture which gave him a pop hit or two for this tune he cowrote with Winans. That collaboration may have been surprising enough, but it's not the one that got tongues wagging most about *Everlasting*.

Lauryn Hill was fresh from a string of hits from The Fugees' *The Score*. Before hitting with her solo debut album, Hill wrote, arranged and produced "On That Day" for Winans. Just as Hill and her Fugee cohorts excel at taking disparate musical elements and undergirding them with a hip-hop base, so she worked "Day" into what could best be described as traditional street gospel: hip-hop's syncopated thrust with the piano, bass and organ coming straight outta church.

Everlasting Love may not have met the sales and radio expectations for a CeCe Winans solo album, but no matter. She made a unified spiritual and creative statement bristling with the currency of sophisticated, urbane style, yet steadied by a clarion call of undying hope and joy.

—*Jamie Lee Rake*

Atlantic 1990
Produced by Sam Taylor and King's X

(52)

FAITH HOPE LOVE BY KING'S X

KING'S X

King's X is arguably the most underrated band of the last two decades—ask any knowledgeable musician or music lover. This general market, progressive power trio has it all: technical chops to die for, soul and spirit dripping from their three-part harmonies, melodic sensibilities that'd make the Beatles smile, and full-on rock 'n' roll hearts that blow away all comers. (The fellas are the highest-ranking hard rockers on this prestigious list, after all.)

As a result, perhaps, of record label indifference, management snafus and bad timing, King's X hasn't jumped over the hump of widespread popularity. And with guitarist Ty Tabor and drummer Jerry Gaskill both pushing 40 and bassist Doug Pinnick at the half-century mark, King's X may never get over.

What's past, however, can't take away from the band's watershed moment, *faith hope love by king's x*—a powerful, focused musical statement released in a somewhat faceless musical year. Here, Pinnick harnesses the spirit of Sly Stone and Otis Redding, wailing and crying at every turn; Tabor at once punishes and caresses the speakers with his unique tone and thick, drop-D tuning (well before grunge made it popular); and Gaskill glues this majestic, careening machine together despite constant, complex time-signature changes on intense tunes like "We Were Born to Be Loved."

More deeply reflective of the band's Christian faith than any of its releases before or since, *faith hope love* discusses spiritual issues in poetic-yet-gut-level fashions. "I'll Never Get Tired of You" is addressed directly to God, as is the searing, six-minute "Moanjam"; MTV staple "It's Love" recognizes Christ's "hand in all"; the delicate "Everywhere I Go" and the militant "We Are Finding Who We Are" address faith's struggle; and the beautiful, acoustic "Legal Kill" is a subtle pro-life rallying cry.

On its charmed third album, King's X demonstrated better than any band to date how melodic metal can happily marry intelligent, biblically informed lyrics. Long may they rock.

—*Dave Urbanski*

Myrrh 1990
Produced by Derri Daugherty and
Steve Hindalong

53

CIRCLE SLIDE

THE CHOIR

Circle Slide, aside from being The Choir's top-selling disc, also marks the end of a certain golden era for the band—an era that began with its 1987 artistic breakthrough, *Chase the Kangaroo*, and continued with *Wide-Eyed Wonder*, its minimalist 1989 follow-up. Hot off those successes, the band retreated to its Neverland Studios to cook up new material, and legend holds that, early in the sessions, guitarist-singer Derri Daugherty fried the speaker in his prized Vox amp. But that didn't stop the band from emerging ten weeks later with its *pièce de résistance*—an album that stands as one of Christian music's rare blends of artistic sensibility and pop accessibility.

"Imagine one perfect circle/above the stratosphere," Daugherty sings on the title track, a shimmering seven-minute cut laden with guitar feedback whose lyrics, by drummer Steve Hindalong, invite us to envision life in the heavenlies, "where lovers hide away/and children cheer." Amid such flights, Hindalong—the band's ever-poetic wordsmith—uses the album to explore get-your-hands-dirty Christianity: the bittersweet affection between husband and wife in "About Love"; the need for redemption in "Restore My Soul"; and his own reality of living in a trailer park (yes, at the height of the band's success) in "If I Had a Yard."

So articulate are the statements, and so elegant the playing (also featuring sax/lyricon-man Dan Michaels and, at this point, four different bass players), that *CCM* readers named The Choir their favorite alternative band in 1991. But, alas, *Circle Slide* would mark a turning point. With middle age beckoning, the band would pack up and move to Nashville, abandoning its golden shimmer of sound in search of a general market deal that never would materialize. Still, *Circle Slide* stands as a milestone in the genre and one of the band's greatest accomplishments.

—*Anthony DeBarros*

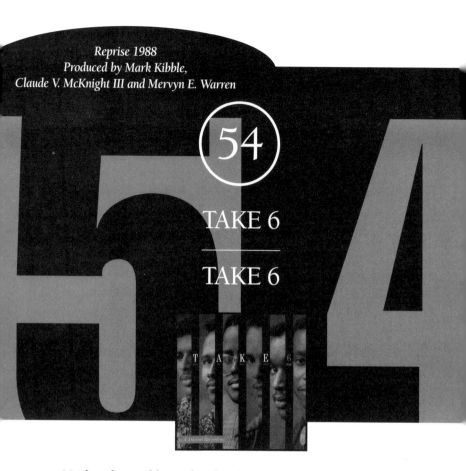

Reprise 1988
Produced by Mark Kibble,
Claude V. McKnight III and Mervyn E. Warren

(54)

TAKE 6

TAKE 6

Neither the world nor the church was necessarily clamoring for a revival of *a cappella* jazz harmonizing in the late 1980s. More than ten years later, *Take 6* still sounds fresh and surprising, luxuriate in an unassumingly sophisticated soulfulness, though not without precedent. A good deal of the sextet's influence came from jazz vocal forbears such as The Hi-Lo's and The Ink Spots. The genius of Take 6 was to fold those sounds into those of jubilee and Golden Age gospel *a cappella* ensembles such as The Fairfield Four, The Harmonizing Four and The Pilgrim Travelers.

It's the old-time, often public domain, repertoire of the latter groups that filled out much of Take 6's premiere offering. "Milky White Way," "David and Goliath," "Get Away, Jordan" and "Mary" were soul gospel standards long before the members of Take 6 locked their larynxes onto them, but here they were imbued with a newfangled harmonic inventiveness to make them sparkle anew. The guys' reading of Thomas A. Dorsey's "If We Ever Needed the Lord Before (We Sure Do Need Him Now)" made for one of the '89 Grammy telecast's musical highlights. It also served as a prelude to the group winning statuettes in both the soul gospel and jazz categories.

Those weren't the only areas in which Take 6 would stake a claim. Throughout the 1990s it was rare to find a male vocal group interviewed on *Soul Train* who didn't acknowledge Take 6 as stylistic mentors, regardless of the raunchiness or righteousness of what they were crooning.

Even if Take 6 may have peaked both commercially and artistically with its first album (their greatest downfall might have been adding so much other instrumentation to their own lustrous pipes on subsequent albums), *Take 6* stands as one of those rare instances when Christ-honoring music brought together a varied constituency of listeners.

—*Jamie Lee Rake*

Broken 1988
Produced by Gene Eugene

55

TEN SONGS BY ADAM AGAIN

ADAM AGAIN

While Adam Again had a funky presence on its '86 debut, *In a New World of Time*, nothing prepared fans for the full-on dance assault of *Ten Songs'* "Beat Peculiar." In addition to the original four-piece, a percussionist enhanced Gene Eugene's mastery of drum machines, and a gospel vocal section added depth and soul to four tracks of the album.

Indeed, this was an unusual alternative record for its time; beat conscious, yet angular, with sections that gave off folk, gospel, jazz and occasionally hard rock vibes. "Who Can Hold Us," with a string arrangement that borrowed from Stevie Wonder and a rich vocal chorus, was not something you'd anticipate from a rock act.

In addition to the lush production values and rich sound tapestry that made *Ten Songs* one of the best Christian records of 1988, Eugene's lyrical observations proved timely and insightful. No less than three songs addressed the issue of living in the world with personal honesty and integrity ("Trouble with Lies," "Eyes Wide Open" and "Every Word I Say"). For Eugene, it was important that he not pretend to be something other than what he was. This reality, together with his refusal to exploit his personal religious experience, may have kept Adam Again's career on the margins of popular expectations within Christian music circles.

"I've Seen Dominoes" addressed families and relationships that were falling down, which, together with a fine, sad cover of "Ain't No Sunshine," began to suggest some of Eugene's own struggles in life. But the album's two bookends were most significant. "Tree House" used a metaphor to describe the exclusivity in some religious and racial groups, and "The Tenth Song" shares a prayer of thanks for the gift of forgiveness in Christ.

Adam Again maintained a strong cult following, and Eugene was one of the Lost Dogs, touching those who came to appreciate his music deeply before his death early in 2000.

—*Brian Quincy Newcomb*

Gotee 1996
Produced by The Gotee Brothers
and Joe Baldridge

56

ERACE

THE GOTEE BROTHERS

Part of what made dc Talk so successful was a melding of Toby McKeehan's fascination with hip-hop with influences by the other members of the group. It doesn't mean, however, that McKeehan didn't need another outlet for all that pent-up funk. Hence The Gotee Brothers.

McKeehan teamed up with his business partners in Gotee Records, Joey Elwood and Todd Collins, to become the "brothers." It could have been simple as a bunch of white boys trading rhymes on the mike with some raw scratching behind them. To the credit of the Gotees, their lone album thus far became much more.

The set's theme of no-colors-in-Christ was articulated most obviously in a cover of War's "Why Can't We Be Friends" with Christafari's Mark Mohr lending a reggae boast to the ditty. Just as Mohr is a white man in a musical form pioneered by those of darker skin, McKeehan poignantly casts his plight as a Caucasian into rap on "Wages of Sin." With a sung chorus by Out of Eden's Lisa Kimmey, the question of godly racial unity is broken down to Cain's plight on "Brother's Keeper." On the album's stunning all-sung apex (and only Christian radio hit), "New South (The Gotee Idyll)," the sin becomes more personal and closer to the heart.

Not everything was so heavy, thankfully. "Sweet Tea" and "Yoknapatawpha (A Mental Mississippi)" relate cultural dichotomies and unities more slyly, less confrontationally. Conversely, "Celia (Queen of the Senseless World)" brings rap's penchant for storytelling deep into sweet heartbreak territory.

The album found a fan in Russell Simmons of Def Jam Recordings and Phat farm boutique fame. But neither the sharpness of the Brothers' rhymes nor their deft interplay of turntables, sampling and "live" instrumentation could get *Erace* far from the ghetto to which Christian rap still appears to be relegated.

—*Jamie Lee Rake*

57

KINGDOM SEEKERS

TWILA PARIS

In the realm of contemporary Christian music, among all the singer/songwriters ever to grace a stage or sing a note, Twila Paris stands out as one of the elite few whose music has made an impact on church hymnody. Three songs off one album alone, *Kingdom Seekers*, are now standards in church hymnals worldwide. In fact, several Paris songs, written in the 15 years since the release of this album, have been translated and sung in many languages around the globe.

"Lamb of God," with its straightforward, confessional lyrics, is so powerful that to this day it can produce goose bumps even when sung *a cappella* by a mediocre singer. "Oh Lamb of God, sweet Lamb of God/I love the Holy Lamb of God/Oh wash me in His precious blood/'Til I am just a lamb of God/My Jesus Christ, the Lamb of God." Paris' pure, unencumbered voice delivers as only one who has experienced these desires can.

"He Is Exalted" and "Faithful Men" are simple, yet profound choruses. One acknowledges God's place in our lives: "He is exalted, the King is exalted on high/I will praise Him...." The other compels believers to "Come and join the reapers called the Kingdom seekers, laying down your life to find it in the end...."

Other popular radio singles off the album include "Runner," "Center of Your Will" and "It All Goes Back to You." Sonically, *Kingdom Seekers* showcases Jonathan David Brown's lush piano and synth-laden arrangements of Paris' skilled, heartfelt songs.

With six Top 40 songs, one of which went to number one on the Christian radio charts, *Kingdom Seekers* proved that popular music need not exclude lyrics that connect with the church, and in the years since, Paris has continued to do just that.

—*Melissa Riddle*

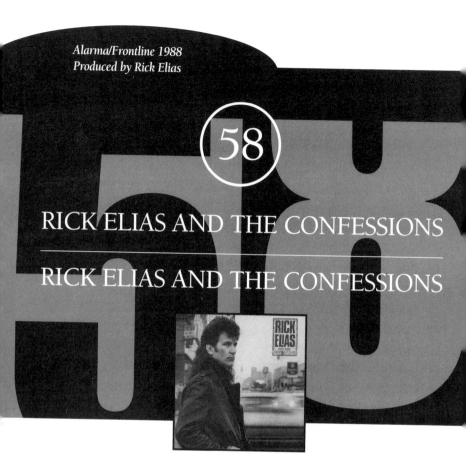

Alarma/Frontline 1988
Produced by Rick Elias

58

RICK ELIAS AND THE CONFESSIONS

RICK ELIAS AND THE CONFESSIONS

Frontline Records, for all its shortcomings, was pretty good at finding some amazing talent in the '80s. From the streets of Southern California came the gritty voice, incredible songwriting and muscular guitar of Rick Elias.

Though new to the Christian music scene, it was obvious that Elias was a long-time veteran of the rock 'n' roll school of hard knocks. His voice sounded as if he had been gargling chipped glass and kerosene for ten years, yet it was evocative and melodically rich. His guitar playing was obviously shaped by years of club gigging and various epochs of influence. But it was probably his lyrical prowess that caught folks off guard the most.

Elias wrote from the perspective of a person with more than his fair share of regrets. His perspective was equally informed by his very relevant faith and his years of experience on the streets. Relationships ("Stripped"), self-destructive behavior ("Streets of Rome," "Stones") and soul-searching ("Without One Word") were couched between bold declarations of faith ("Confession of Love," "The Word Is Love") to great effect. *Rick Elias and the Confessions* was a gut-level expression of real-life faith amidst the wreckage of the western world.

Elias rocked with the swagger of Bruce Springsteen, and his innate sense of melody brought accessibility to his rock and power-pop tunes. His concerts became the stuff of legend to the few who had the chance to see them. Unfortunately, since the Christian music industry really didn't have a niche for thoughtful and mature roots-rock, Elias fell through the cracks as alt bands sprang up around his feet like weeds.

Eventually Elias would go on to lead the Ragamuffin Band, and even make a splash in the pop world by producing, writing and playing for the Tom Hanks film *That Thing You Do!*

—*John J. Thompson*

Light 1972
Produced by Bill Cole

59

SOULFULLY

ANDRAÉ CROUCH & THE DISCIPLES

The cover said a lot about this record: the four key members of Andraé Crouch's Disciples photographed on a set of railroad tracks, looking the way black people looked in 1972—Afro hairstyles, bright funky clothes and a healthy amount of pride in their faces. The back cover said the rest: the band as it appeared live, fleshed out with a drummer and two guitarists—all three Caucasians—playing live on Johnny Carson's *Tonight Show*. Railroad tracks or NBC, it was clear: this band was going places.

Those photos also told the truth about the music inside. Though AC&D had recorded two previous albums for Light, they were arranged for the type of white audience listening to inspirational radio for whom Evie was rock 'n' roll. *Soulfully* marked the first time the group's trend-setting sounds began to be captured in the studio.

Sly & the Family Stone it wasn't—but a close listen to the arrangements for *Soulfully* reveals that *somebody* was listening to that band as well as Motown and the emerging Philadelphia Sound. Guitars played through wah-wah pedals and "fuzz-tone" distortion units, electric sitars and the aforementioned Philly Soul strings made this album almost as fun to listen to as it was to experience AC&D in concert.

Though arguably not the strongest collection of songs on any one Crouch album, *Soulfully* featured a number of tunes that would become staples in the group's live repertoire for years ("Satisfied," "He Proved His Love to Me," "You Don't Know What You're Missing") and two that are among the best loved and most covered in his catalog ("Through It All" and "It Won't Be Long").

Higher heights were yet to be scaled for this band (see number 24), but truth is, this album was a particularly tasty slice of soul food back in 1972, and still sounds great today.

—*Thom Granger*

60

PAGES OF LIFE, CHAPTERS I & II

FRED HAMMOND AND RADICAL FOR CHRIST

The history of modern gospel music—that is, the fusion of traditional gospel vocal textures with more earthy, dense R&B rhythms—can be traced to the innovations of two men: Kirk Franklin and Fred Hammond. While Franklin boasts the knack for grabbing attention (especially with mainstream music critics), Hammond can rightfully be called the foundation. The musical moves he made as founder of Commissioned laid the groundwork that made Franklin's bold experiments possible.

With *Pages of Life*, Hammond sought to break down barriers in gospel—and in his own career and spiritual life. Prior to its 1998 release, he referred to the record as his equivalent of Stevie Wonder's *Songs in the Key of Life*. Hammond's self-stated goal was to craft a work that was deeply personal and epic in scope and texture, yet not so haughty that it lost sight of its groove, or the listener it was intended to move.

Hammond succeeded using a double-barrelled strategy. At first uncertain whether to record a live or a studio album, Hammond opted for both, hammering out a two-disc album that proved his mastery in each area. As if to reinforce this fact, he led off both "chapters" with the same song, "Let the Praise Begin." It's difficult to say which is the better version, for each excels; the studio track throbs with precise rhythm and punchy harmony, while the live track swings and sways as if to suggest the give-and-take between Hammond's choir and the audience. The studio side also contains one of Hammond's most stirring ballads, "Don't Pass Me By"—a song where Hammond confronts the fear that Christ might be too busy to answer the prayers of a lone (and lonely) believer. Hammond's refrain is a direct cry from his own heart to Jesus' ear.

—*Lou Carlozo*

Qwest 1990
Produced by Michael J. Powell, Teddy Riley,
Bernard Bell and Marvin Winans.
CoProduced by The Winans

61

RETURN

THE WINANS

"The Winans made a go-go record!" I enthused to a college friend on the phone.

The truth behind "It's Time" was more than that. Producer Teddy Riley fashioned for the veteran brotherly contemporary soul gospel quartet an ingenious fusion of Washington D.C.'s tribally percussive R&B permutation of go-go with the "new jack swing" sound Riley made popular with hits by Guy and Johnny Kemp, among others. It gave The Winans a top-five R&B hit that was even bigger at Christian pop radio.

Riley and other producers refurbished The Winans' sound for a broader audience than ever. Stevie Wonder offered harmonica licks and a vocal cameo on the breezy "Everyday the Same." Kenny G gave it up on the sax for the sumptuously down-tempo "When You Cry."

"Don't Leave Me" took the neo-swing beat into a more fleshed out realm, whereas "A Friend" delivered a smoother sheen to The Winans in a dance mode. The rhythmically fidgety confession of "This Time It's Personal" split the difference on breakdance-ready electro-funk and smooth jazz with a tropical flair.

Concerned as the siblings were with the state of their own and others' souls, unity was on their minds, too. "Together We Stand" could be taken as a call to abolish the church's denominational and racial barriers to stand for truth or a broad-based ballad to all of moral conscience. The same kind of vocal lushness and melodic stateliness pervades on the hymn-like "Gonna Be Alright" and "Wherever I Go."

A mite heavy on the slow numbers in its second half, *Return* still stands as an album of creative diversity and thematic balance. It gave Carvin, Marvin, Michael and Ron their first gold record and a platform for sharing the gospel on R&B outlets beyond their Sunday programming. That they expanded their fan base in contemporary Christian circles and contributed to the development of '90s adult R&B ices the cake.

—*Jamie Lee Rake*

NewPax 1981
Produced by Daniel Amos and Thom Roy

62

ALARMA!

DANIEL AMOS

If *Horrendous Disc* caught Christian music fans off guard (see next entry), *Alarma!* was a wake-up call akin to someone putting a pot over your head and beating it with a wooden spoon.

In the years awaiting *Disc's* release, Terry Taylor & Co. had begun to take more of their cues from the emerging new wave scene and mainstream artists like the Talking Heads and Elvis Costello. Forging ahead, D.A. was intent on making the Christian message available in music that spoke to current rock fans, thus eclipsing the five to ten year "cultural lag" that seemed to plague so much Christian music produced by major labels. Taylor and D.A. are the mother ship that made Christian alternative rock possible, and *Alarma!* is the record that opened the door.

Taylor had always been a strong melodic writer, but the lyrical progression that made *Disc* feel cutting edge was catching wildfire on *Alarma!* Trusting the "Ghost of the Heart," and the innate intelligence of his fans, Taylor believed listeners would get the message he was sharing in rich metaphors and bold, literate images without showing them his cards at the end of each hand. Thus, the record stands up as a bold witness to faith in the message of the gospel, but is never preachy.

We are invited to see the truth, and not have our understandings limited or "Colored By" trendy theology and powerful ministers. And Taylor's own efforts to share the gospel in artful rock music is considered in "Through the Speakers" and "Big Time/Big Deal." If we're going to speak to the world as Jesus did, says Taylor, we need to "Hit Them" with love, which also creates a social responsibility ("Faces to the Window"). It's a theme that will surface again and again in D.A. as they break with convention and make ever more relevant Christian rock music.

—*Brian Quincy Newcomb*

Solid Rock 1980
Produced by Daniel Amos and Mike Stone

63

HORRENDOUS DISC

DANIEL AMOS

By the time *Horrendous Disc* reached retailers, fans of the original Maranatha! Music "Cowboys from Outer Space" Jesus music band had begun to think the title was a reference to the ordeal it took to get the record out. They'd been hearing the title track, "Hound of Heaven" and "I Love You #19" at concerts, and for country music fans the "horrendous" had become synonymous with the band's move into rock 'n' roll.

Terry Taylor & Co. were never country enthusiasts (you can hear Beatles and Beach Boy influences in their earliest work), but the cowboy shtick worked with the band's warped comic sensibilities. By the time they joined up with Larry Norman's Solid Rock, they were ready to be taken seriously, evolving in similar directions as The Eagles toward an L.A. sound and big-production, commercial pop/rock songs. Listening two decades later, *Disc* is an accessible, fun-easy listen. But the move from country and toward broader lyrical themes made the whole effort seem radical within the Christian music context.

Opening with the loud distorted guitar line of "I Love You" by Jerry Chamberlain, *Disc* was something brand new. In a subculture that liked references to Jesus up-front and center, D.A.'s more literate approach was considered by some to be a compromise, but looking back it's easy to see that the message of God's love made known in Christ is there in each and every song. God is that "Hound," the seeker of souls, the "Sky King (Out Across the Sky)," who is "On the Line," calling long distance with a message "especially for you."

The band's fascination with end-times themes continued on the title track and "(Near-sighted Girl with Approaching) Tidal Wave," but D.A. was moving on, presenting the good news message in a medium that would speak to nonbelievers. And they'd only just begun to change.

—*Brian Quincy Newcomb*

NewSong 1976
Produced by Buck Herring

64

LOVE BROKE THRU

PHIL KEAGGY

Already a renowned guitarist with three celebrated records as part of the Ohio-based power-trio Glass Harp, Phil Keaggy was ready to show the world what he could do as a witness of his Christian faith when he moved to Ithaca, New York, to join a community led by Scott Ross. His first solo outing, *What a Day,* gave the artist a chance to express his own identity (and play all the instruments) on songs of heartfelt praise. For *Love Broke Thru,* Keaggy created a state-of-the-times Christian pop/rock statement at a time when Christian music production values tended to lag behind mainstream peers. It remains a fan favorite.

The bright pop melodies of the title track, written by two Christian music veterans (Keith Green and Randy Stonehill) and Todd Fishkind, "Take Me Closer" and "Just the Same," established Keaggy's vocal talent. However, for fans of Keaggy's guitar heroics, best experienced in live concert settings, "Time" was the quintessential rock track, edgy and expansive enough in theme to allow extended improvisation.

In the studio, Keaggy and Buck Herring had turned to two of the strongest session players around, bassist Leland Sklar and drummer Jim Gordon, while 2nd Chapter of Acts came in to add background vocals with a still rocking but soon prodigal Mylon LeFevre. Keaggy, who had worked on Paul Clark's albums, would go on to join 2nd Chapter on tour, and record the live *How the West Was One* (number 93).

Keaggy's natural guitar talents, melodic sensibilities and heart for God's people would make him a prominent figure in the growing Christian music industry, demonstrated by a later collaborating with guitarists Scott Denté (Out of the Grey) and Wes King. It is very likely that Keaggy's monumental instrumental capabilities, together with his gentle, self-deprecating humor and easygoing nature, helped an industry that found mainstream rock forms suspect to embrace the electric guitar.

—*Brian Quincy Newcomb*

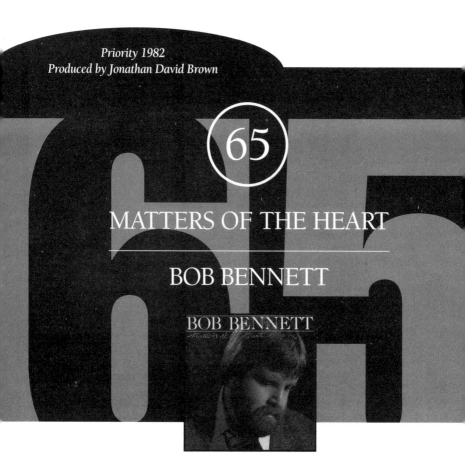

Priority 1982
Produced by Jonathan David Brown

65

MATTERS OF THE HEART

BOB BENNETT

Ask a hundred music fans about their favorite Christian singer/song-writers and you'll get a long list. Ask the same question of veteran Christian singer/songwriters and you'll get a much shorter list...and chances are that Bob Bennett's name will be on it. Bennett may not have become a household name, but his artistry is revered by those in the know.

After his 1979 debut on the Maranatha! Music label, Bennett signed with Priority Records, CBS's short-lived foray into Christian music. *Matters of the Heart*, Bennett's only release on that label, was rated by *CCM* as the top album of 1982.

Bennett's deeply personal lyrics evoked real life—his life—from the seemingly mundane ("A Song About Baseball") to the spiritually sublime ("Come and See"). He was the rare Christian songwriter who boldly and artfully wrote songs that honestly reflected the messier side of life. Jonathan David Brown's production supported Bennett's mellow delivery with a punchy acoustic-folk sound (à la James Taylor), full and rich.

Bennett himself has described his career as "critically accepted but commercially mediocre." A sad but true statement, which might best be balanced with a lyric from this album's title track: "There are just some things that numbers can't measure in matters of the heart."

—*John W. Styll*

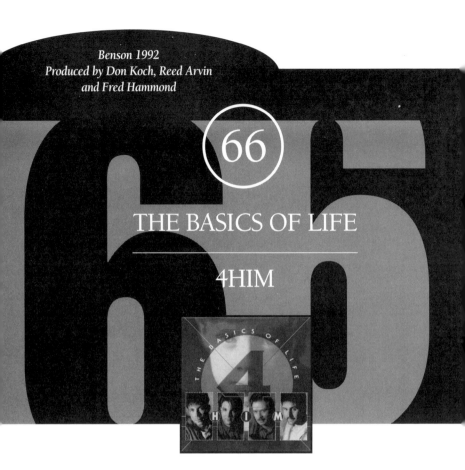

Benson 1992
Produced by Don Koch, Reed Arvin and Fred Hammond

66

THE BASICS OF LIFE

4HIM

Mark, Marty, Andy and Kirk. No, they weren't Christian music's first boy band nor would their choreography ever set any heart racing. But these four veterans of the touring group Truth brought crowds to their feet with the powerhouse vocals and unique blend found on their 1990 self-titled debut. After garnering a Dove Award for New Artist of the Year the following spring, 4HIM released *Face the Nation* to the glee of its growing cadre of fans.

But it was the group's third album, *The Basics of Life*, which hit the ball out of the park, combining all the strengths of previous efforts with a convincing thematic appeal to return to the traditional values of days gone by. In fact, the men of 4HIM even invited their fathers to join them on the Mark Harris/Don Koch-penned "Built on Amazing Grace," using the classic hymn as a bridge not only for the song but as a connection between the present and the past. Harris, who cowrote seven of the 12 tracks, focuses on lyrics that don't simply encourage the church but admonish listeners to think about—and act on—their faith.

With a triad of diverse producers—Koch, Reed Arvin and gospel legend Fred Hammond— and four strong vocalists up front, it would be easy for this album to lack cohesion, but just the opposite proves true. Whether led by the soothing and smooth-toned voice of Harris ("When It's Time to Go"), Andy Chrisman's super-tenor ("When It Comes to Livin' "), the famously flexible falsetto of Marty Magehee ("Voice of God") or the driving power of Kirk Sullivan ("Freedom"), each song flows effortlessly into the next.

Perhaps it's a result of great sequencing, perhaps it's just one more reminder of how perfectly these four unique voices complement one another. Regardless, this album works as well when highlighting an individual as it does when the four singers combine for their still-dazzling harmonic magic.

—April Hefner

Exit 1984
Produced by Charlie Peacock

67

LIE DOWN IN THE GRASS

CHARLIE PEACOCK

Charlie Peacock's role as keyboardist on the excellent debut from Vector, *Mannequin Virtue*, did not prepare one for his unique musical and lyrical voice. A perpetrator of pure pop, Peacock's own music was infused with an eclectic sensibility and a demanding creativity and level of musicianship that drew on an awareness of jazz and world beat.

Featuring players from other Exit bands, the 77's and Vector (Aaron Smith and Jimmy Abegg, who would go on to play in Rich Mullins' Ragamuffin Band), Peacock delivered accessible melodies in a sophisticated format that challenged the listener with layers of fun, off-beat surprises. Peacock would later move to Nashville and produce winning albums for Margaret Becker and Out of the Grey, but here he developed a quirky, literate presence that suggested mainstream success while speaking in a voice that connected with Christians who had a broader musical experience.

In bold metaphors and vivid imagery, Peacock spoke to the innocence of childlike faith in "Young in Heart" (on the general market A&M version), "One, Two, Three (That's Okay)" and the amazing title track, which encouraged the listener to experience God in the simple wonder of creation. He bridged the distance between Christians and nonbelievers in "Whole Lot Different/Whole Lot the Same" and captured the common need for peace and hope in "Who Is Not Afraid?"

That which is broken in the world is faced in helpful ways on "Love Doesn't Get Better," "It's Gone, It's Over," "Lost in Translation" and "Turned On an Attitude." But even though "The world had been selling me a lie," God's redeeming action is felt in "Till You Caught My Eye."

Peacock's strong songs and impeccable musical effort on this debut not only suggested his own talented future but pointed the way for Christian artists who wanted to engage the world in a dialogue about faith, hope and the meaning of life.

—*Brian Quincy Newcomb*

Forefront 1992
Produced by Dave Bainbridge

68

THE BOOK OF KELLS

IONA

Iona's hybrid of progressive rock and Celtic folk music has been like oxygen for those believers who cut their musical teeth on the epic, decidedly noncommercial songs of progsters such as Yes and Genesis. Like those bands, Iona has been unafraid to explore intricate musicality, sometimes stretching compositions near the quarter-hour mark—a quality of adventure that has captured a loyal fan base.

Though the Iona catalog is universally excellent (with five studio and two live albums thus far), *The Book of Kells*, Iona's second album, represents an early pinnacle in the group's career. A concept work, its name is taken from an eighth-century manuscript of the four

Gospels illuminated by brilliant drawings and calligraphy. In the course of 72 minutes, *Kells* takes listeners on a journey through the Book and, along the way, the character of Christ.

Its scenes are stunning: In "Luke—The Calf," a melancholy flute plays against a backing of strings and the sound of waves crashing against a shore, evoking the Lord's sacrifice on the cross. The 12-minute "Matthew—The Man" captures Christ's humanity as singer Joanne Hogg acknowledges "the tears that salt the earth/the wounds that bleed the land." And a 32-minute suite of instrumentals illustrates Christ's temptation in the wilderness, his arrest and resurrection.

What makes this album such a gem is the immense authority that the band wields in addressing its subject. *Kells* features a classic Iona lineup: core members Hogg on vocals and Dave Bainbridge on guitar and keyboards, plus sax/woodwind player David Fitzgerald (who would leave shortly after the album's release). Also on board: drummers Terl Bryant and Frank Van Essen, piper Troy Donockley and bass/stick player Nick Beggs (formerly of Euro-pop '80s band Kajagoogoo). Without exception, their playing continually evokes the majesty and wonder of the Creator in a way that few albums have, before or since.

—*Anthony DeBarros*

Dayspring 1989
Produced by Randy Thomas and
Bob Carlisle

69

LONG WAY FROM PARADISE

ALLIES

After stints in early bands like Good News and Psalm 150, Bob
Carlisle spent years playing nightclubs in cover bands to make ends
meet. Likewise, Randy Thomas cut his teeth in the Sweet Comfort
Band, and was looking for a band to believe in again. Old friends,
Carlisle said goodbye to the bars and the two talked. With the addition of fellow Southern Cal musicians Matthew Chapman on bass
and Jimmy Erickson on drums (and originally, Sam Scott on keyboards), Allies was born.

Two albums for Light introduced the band, but things amped up
when Word signed the band to its Dayspring label. 1987's *Shoulder
to Shoulder* was the first Allies record to be produced by Carlisle and

Thomas alone, and that, coupled with a new emphasis on the kind of R&B-inflected pop that Hall & Oates were taking to the bank in the mid-'80s, seemed to make all the difference. Three of the album's tunes charted on Christian radio, emboldening the band to take it to the next level.

With no less than five Top 10-charting songs amongst its grab bag of Carlisle-Thomas originals and one fine cover ("Crying in the Chapel"), *Long Way from Paradise* was Allies' masterpiece, one that seemed to challenge its growing audience to grow with them and, uh, have a little fun.

That may have also been the problem. In a market rife with serious evangelical intent, *LWFP* (and Carlisle's vocals in particular) celebrated great rock 'n' roll as much as it did the spiritual, though it certainly did plenty of the latter. With lyric nods to Muddy Waters and musical references to an encyclopedia of rock history, Allies just sounded like they were having too much fun with too much rock attitude.

Funny thing is, the same combo had worked wonders for Larry Norman a generation before, which may have been the other problem. The label insisted on marketing Allies to '80s kids, who weren't remotely interested in retooled classic rock and blues, however cleverly executed. After two more great but less consistent albums, Allies was over. Carlisle and Thomas grabbed the biggest brass ring of their careers with "Butterfly Kisses" in '96, and guys like me wish they'd make music like this again.

—*Thom Granger*

Star Song 1994
Produced by Steve Taylor and
Peter Furler

70

GOING PUBLIC

NEWSBOYS

For the Newsboys, the latter half of the '90s saw an artistic coming-of-age. Feisty Australian lads, their first record was released in 1988. It was not until 1992, however, when *Not Ashamed* was unveiled, that these boys really started to become men.

Prior to that pivotal record, Newsboys were routinely pegged as a derivative, energetic diversion that was more fun to watch in concert than listen to on record. For *Not Ashamed*, the very notable Steve Taylor was invited to the party as producer and cowriter, and the ascent began. Critics, listeners and probably the band itself were taken off guard by fully realized, smart songs and (surprise!) an emerging style all their own.

In hindsight, the alternative pop of *Not Ashamed* was an excellent setup for the more polished *Going Public* that followed two years later. The band—then comprised of Peter Furler, Jody Davis, John James, Kevin Mills and Dunny Phillips—had got its feet wet on the former and took a most graceful swan dive with the latter. *Going Public* was a more confident and mature statement that delivered quite a few now-classic tracks, especially the shimmering "Spirit Thing" and the shining "Shine." The record also broke the bank, becoming the first Newsboys disc to be certified gold and became the calling card that led to fully realized mainstream distribution via Virgin Records in 1996.

Since *Going Public*, Newsboys have remained in the public eye as one of the most visible Christian acts. They went on to prove that Steve Taylor was not the only wizard behind the curtain (he only stuck around for one more record), successfully survived the departure of lead singer James and pulled off a tour in 2000 that involved an inflatable dome stage. Forging into the 21st century, Newsboys appear to have plenty more headlines to deliver.

—*Robert Mineo*

Dayspring 1990
Produced by John and Dino Elefante

71

BEYOND BELIEF

PETRA

Yes, Petra means rock and yes, this group, originally founded in 1972 by guitarist/songwriter Bob Hartman, has done just that for its entire existence. Among the most successful Christian rock bands ever, these fellows have been able to justify chasing musical trends with the guise of maintaining a relevant ministry. Despite all the shape shifting, the group has managed to hit a few artistic bull's eyes along the way. *Beyond Belief* is one of them.

At this point, former lead singer Greg X. Volz had been gone for a while and his replacement, John Schlitt, who still remains in place today, had fully settled in. The corporate rock sound that Volz helped develop (see *More Power to Ya*, number 98) conceded to the arena, "hair band" rock of the day. The band whipped up an appealing mix of bombastic stadium anthems and catchy pop that was visually enhanced by a few high-octane hairdos.

Schlitt, who had notched a measure of mainstream success prior to Petra (with Head East), was up to the task, and led the charge through battle cries such as "Armed and Dangerous" and fist pumping sing-alongs like the title track. There were a few softer moments, as in the power ballad "Love," but in general this record roared, smashing irrepressible melodic hooks deep into the cranium. True to form, the lyrical message stuck to spiritual matters.

Ten years later it is hard to deny that *Beyond Belief* is great fun to listen to. It eventually earned Petra its first Grammy Award and was the first of a trilogy (including subsequent releases *Unseen Power* and *Wake-Up Call*) to display some of the sharpest songwriting ever from Hartman, who currently maintains a behind-the-scenes role in the band.

—Robert Mineo

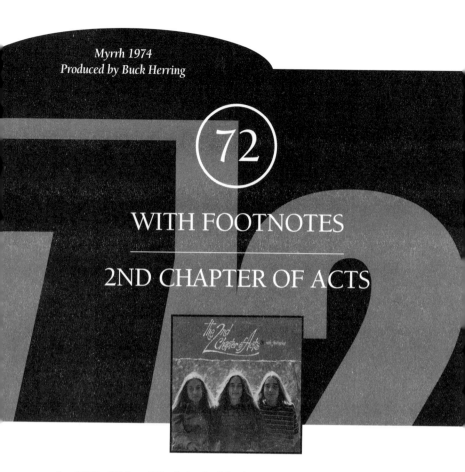

Myrrh 1974
Produced by Buck Herring

72

WITH FOOTNOTES

2ND CHAPTER OF ACTS

In 1970, Walter Ward died of leukemia, two years after his wife Elizabeth's death from a brain tumor. With four children still at home, two went to live with the eldest brother, but Nelly and Matthew, aged 14 and 12, went to live with their oldest sister Annie and her husband of a year and a half, Buck Herring.

At the same time, songs about her new-found faith began to pour from Annie's heart, and were soon fleshed out with harmonies from Nelly and Matthew, and the 2nd Chapter of Acts was birthed. A recording of a song called "Jesus Is," recorded on Matthew's 13th birthday, came to the attention of Pat Boone, who likewise brought it to the attention of MGM Records, who released it as a single. Another one followed, but few paid much attention.

One who did was Barry McGuire, himself a new convert eager to share his faith, who took the trio on the road with him, cutting tracks with Herring in the studio between gigs. Annie and her siblings were doing the same, with the help of Buck and some "A" session players in Los Angeles.

Eventually Herring met Billy Ray Hearn, a Word Records executive who had recently launched the Myrrh label to record the new songs of the "Jesus People." Hearn signed McGuire, whose 1973 *Seeds* album featured the trio on background vocals, and then the 2nd Chapter of Acts, on the strength of Annie's remarkable "Easter Song."

That's the story. The album is even better. Featuring impeccable playing by Michael Omartian on keyboards, Michael Been on bass, Jim Gordon on drums and others, the real stars of *With Footnotes* were Annie, Nelly and Matthew. Annie was a composer who so impacted Omartian's life that he wrote a song about her for a mainstream album ("Annie the Poet"). Matthew sang with more blue-eyed soul at 13 than most do in a lifetime. The sound of the three together was like hearing the angels themselves. At least, I hope the angels sound that good.

—*Thom Granger*

GospoCentric 1993
Produced by Rodney Frazier
and Arthur Dyer

73

KIRK FRANKLIN AND THE FAMILY

KIRK FRANKLIN AND THE FAMILY

Kirk Franklin had already made a name for himself, writing for and performing with choirs local to him, such as The Dallas-Fort Worth Mass Choir, at the time he and his friends in his Family chorus signed as the second act on the fledgling GospoCentric label.

A right time/right place/right song confluence worked incredibly in Franklin's and The Family's favors. That number, "Why We Sing," a contemporary reworking of "His Eye Is on the Sparrow" felt like an oasis whenever it came on the air, especially on the R&B outlets where it became a surprise crossover hit.

Beyond that song, Franklin knew how to mix things up to please a wide gospel public. Where "He Can Handle It" traded in a little rap for youngsters, "Call on the Lord" had the traditional feel older listeners may have favored. "The Family Worship Medley" worked a contemporary praise vibe, while "Speak to Me" revealed a tropical/calypso strain sounding like a furtherance of a similar vein pioneered by Thomas Whitfield. "Silver & Gold" (the record company's original pick for a breakout single) and "Till We Meet Again" spun balladic bliss similar to that of "Why We Sing."

Franklin wasn't shy about capitalizing on his handsome looks, but neither did he flinch from telling his preconversion testimony of thug life as an inspiration to young people wanting God to work in their lives for personal reformation. *Kirk Franklin and The Family* was a diverse album by an act ready for the limelight.

Franklin's platinum-winning streak would continue with a couple of other albums with The Family and as a mentor to another young choir who would cross over with their own kind of gospel funk, God's Property. Those same choirs would not long thereafter litigate against Franklin. That setback, however, is no detriment to his achievement in bringing a creatively rendered gospel update to masses who might not have otherwise heard the gospel sung so relevantly to them.

—*Jamie Lee Rake*

Sparrow 1986
Produced by Billy Smiley and White Heart

74

DON'T WAIT FOR THE MOVIE

WHITE HEART

For the members of White Heart, *Don't Wait for the Movie* couldn't have come at a better time.

From its beginnings in 1981, White Heart had always seemed to be in a state of flux. The only constants, Billy Smiley and Mark Gersmehl (who shared keyboard, songwriting, vocal and sometimes guitar duties), were surrounded at first by a very capable cast of characters: vocalist Steve Green (who went on to greater success in the inspirational field), guitarist Dann Huff, bassist Gary Lunn and drummer David Huff.

Then the changes began: that very year, Scott Douglas replaced Green; in '84, Gordon Kennedy replaced the guitar-playing Huff; and in '85 Chris McHugh replaced the drumming Huff.

Then, in January 1985, Scott Douglas (real name: Scott Mathieson) was convicted of charges of sexual abuse and sentenced to a Tennessee prison. The band, battered but determined to carry on, called on Rick Florian, formerly a roadie with the band, to step up and take the lead vocal duties.

It was with this lineup that the band recorded this, their first and most successful album to date, for Sparrow Records. Although it did have its serious moments, for the most part *Don't Wait* was a fun album, perfect for a band that was in dire need of some fun in their lives and career. Gersmehl, Smiley and Kennedy shared the thrust of the songwriting duties, while Florian quickly settled into the role of animated front man.

But even in the midst of reclaiming their place in Christian music, another change took place, this time with original member Lunn bowing out, and a young Indiana man named Tommy Sims taking his place for this tour and the next two albums. The rock-funk spark Sims (who would later team with Kennedy and Wayne Kirkpatrick to pen the Grammy-winning song "Change the World" for Eric Clapton) brought to the band was evident in the long-form video that documented the *Don't Wait* tour.

—*Lucas W. Hendrickson*

Dayspring 1979
Produced by Michael Omartian

75

ONE MORE SONG FOR YOU

IMPERIALS

In existence since 1964, the Imperials have been on the scene longer and have released more albums (40+) than any other artist or group on the "100 Greatest" list. And they are the only group on the list whose career includes a stint as backup singers for Elvis Presley (!).

Armond Morales, the venerable (and no doubt tired) bass singer, is the only original member of the group. The amazing list of Imperials' alumni includes Russ Taff, Jake Hess, Gary McSpadden, Jim Murray, Ron Hemby, Jimmy Lee Sloas, Paul Smith, Sherman Andrus, Terry Blackwood, Jonathan Pierce and even Larry Gatlin. Given enough time, *everybody* could have been an Imperial!

In the late '60s, the Imperials' sound began to evolve from its Southern gospel roots to a more commercial pop style. Producer Gary S. Paxton modernized their sound in 1975 with the album *No Shortage*. The addition of Russ Taff as lead singer in 1976 and Chris Christian as producer completed that transition. But it was *One More Song for You*, their 27th album, that marked a major turning point for the Imperials. One key reason was that Michael Omartian became their producer and arranger, giving them unprecedented credibility and the sound that kicked in the afterburners at the peak of their popularity.

Michael and his wife, Stormie, wrote five of the album's nine songs, including the title track. Michael is also listed as cowriter of a sixth song—"I'm Forgiven" (which turned out to be the only track from the album to reach number 1 on the *CCM* charts). Omartian had such influence on the sound of the album that he was pictured on the back cover with the four singers as though he was a member of the group!

—*John W. Styll*

Myrrh 1989
Produced by Mark Heard

RETURN TO PARADISE
RANDY STONEHILL

(76)

Randy Stonehill's acoustic-dominated *Return to Paradise* stuck out like a rootsy, organic sore thumb in a late '80s musical landscape ruled by hair-metal bands and the mainstream jangle of college-rock bands like R.E.M. and The Cure. The genius of this "sequel" to Stonehill's most famous work, 1976's *Welcome to Paradise* (number 13), is its arresting timelessness. *Return to Paradise* was depth-filled and honest in 1989—and would still outshine the competition on today's taste-making, sophisticated radio programs like *World Cafe.*

Stonehill—guided here by the masterful production of the late, great Mark Heard—makes his finger-picked Martin acoustic sing like an accompanying voice to his own plaintive cries. A feast for the ears, Heard capitalizes on the back-to-basics vibe by adding fretless and acoustic basses, pedal and lap steel guitars, fiddles, violas and percussion to the mix as well as his accordion and mandolin sounds and Phil Keaggy's classical and 12-string work.

The true highlights are Stonehill's lyrics, full of vivid storytelling ("Starlings," "Christmas at Denny's," "Weight of the Sky"), social justice ("Stand Like Steel"), faith ("True Blood," "Ready to Go,") and a bang-up cover of Heard's "Strong Hand of Love."

—*Dave Urbanski*

Street Level 1994
Produced by Buddy & Julie Miller

INVISIBLE GIRL
JULIE MILLER

77

After three exceptional, if uneven, albums for Myrrh, 1994's *Invisible Girl* was Miller's swan song in Christian music, and it is a masterpiece.

It is easy for fans of picture-perfect pop to dismiss Julie Miller. Her voice, while tuneful and pitch-perfect, is also breathy, girlish, slightly slurred and always on the edge of breaking. She also writes songs that refuse to be easily categorized, flirting with Appalachian twang and Memphis soul, New York sophistication and back-porch stomp, but always making them distinctly and uniquely her own.

Close to a concept album, *Invisible Girl* is a kind of open letter to the margins of the contemporary Christian music audience, full of songs that, like Christ's parable of the great banquet, invite the broken, outcasts, crippled, poor and unwanted to the kingdom. Inspired in large measure by interaction with fans—including the victim of horrible abuse in the title—the songs on *Invisible Girl* alternately offer gentle comfort and wild, joyous hope to the "least of these," somehow finding a way to still be playful and charming in the midst of suffering. "Come all of you ragged and unshod/Come and be embraced and loved by God" ("Nobody's Child").

That ability to reach into the heart of despair and still offer grace is what makes Julie Miller essential listening.

—*Dwight Ozard*

Word/Epic (1999)
Produced by Brent Bourgeois
and Loren Balman

STREAMS

VARIOUS ARTISTS

78

A multiartist concept album released during the summer of 1999 when various artist soundtracks ruled the *Billboard* charts, *Streams* seemed to have many things working against it. At first glance, it could have looked like the Christian market was merely trying to tap into the trend of the day the only way it knew how (and without using the title *WoW*).

It only takes a few seconds of listening to the opener, however (Cindy Morgan's contemplative "Job"), and a few seconds of perusing the exquisitely designed CD booklet, to realize the one thing this compilation has over others of its ilk: pure, unadulterated excellence.

This concept album, a labor of love for producer Brent Bourgeois and Word executive Loren Balman, tackles the reality of crises in our lives. It features some inspired casting, including Clannad vocalist Maire Brennan with former Doobie Brothers vocalist Michael McDonald on a reworking of the Peter Gabriel classic, "Don't Give Up"; veteran vocal pop group 4HIM with Yes' Jon Anderson on "The Only Thing I Need"; and Brit-popsters Delirious? with Amy Grant on "Find Me in the River."

It also features some outstanding individual performances, such as the three-song pathway of "Breathe," "Sanctuary" and "Hold On," which may be the best performances in the careers of Leigh Nash, Chris Rodriguez and Michelle Tumes, respectively.

—*Lucas W. Hendrickson*

Star Song 1991
Produced by Richard Souther

SANCTUARY

TWILA PARIS

(79)

When Twila Paris set out to make a record intended for use in personal worship, she had already recorded ten albums and racked up a slew of inspirational radio hits. So how would this new endeavor differ from the tried-and-true formula of her previous recordings? According to Paris, she wanted to record a disc that would create a certain atmosphere for the listener, offering calming, soothing music with an entirely "vertical" focus. In October 1991, *Sanctuary* fulfilled that aim.

Produced and arranged by instrumentalist/composer Richard Souther, *Sanctuary* was immediately well received, garnering two number one singles: "The Joy of the Lord" and "Come Worship the Lord." In addition, this album earned Paris her first Dove Award in 1992 (for Praise and Worship Album of the Year), and eventually spawned both a video and a book Paris coauthored with Robert Webber. Four instrumental tracks—including one original and three Paris standards—add to the uniqueness of this disc, as does a Brazilian version of "He Is Exalted."

While recording an album designed solely for personal worship doesn't seem at all out of the ordinary in today's saturated worship music market, in 1991 it was not at all commonplace. As a result, *Sanctuary* will probably go down in history as one of the pioneering discs of the modern worship movement.

—*Laura Harris*

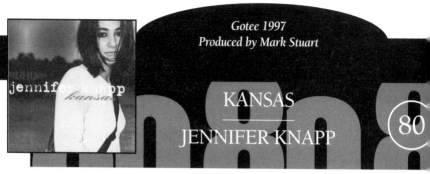

Gotee 1997
Produced by Mark Stuart

KANSAS
JENNIFER KNAPP

80

After several years spent launching urban acts into the largely white-washed Christian music industry, many were surprised when Gotee Records' founder Toby McKeehan introduced his latest find in 1997—a young Caucasian female who sang straight-ahead, acoustic rock songs. But never fear—McKeehan hadn't lost his touch or his devotion to a counterculture. The then 23-year-old Jennifer Knapp didn't fit into any predictable formulas—this was a girl proud of her callused fingers and not afraid to reveal her broken spirit.

On her debut, titled *Kansas* after her home state, Knapp unleashed a talent raw with emotion and a voice that could deliver it equally well live and in the studio. The songs, nine of which were self-penned, reflect her struggle, her questions, her fears of not being good enough and her love for a God she has found faithful.

Produced by Audio Adrenaline's Mark Stuart, *Kansas* boasts five cuts that landed in the Top 10 on Christian radio, including "Undo Me," a plea for personal forgiveness bound tightly with a need for spiritual undoing, and the rough-and-tumble "Romans" in which Knapp calls to mind a Sheryl Crow/Shawn Colvin combination.

Kansas met with rave reviews and commercial success, not to mention landing Jennifer Knapp the first two Dove Awards in what was sure to be a robust career.

—*April Hefner*

Word 1996
Produced by Brent Bourgeois and Craig Hansen

81

LISTEN
CINDY MORGAN

At first, Cindy Morgan was expected to be Christian music's next dance-pop queen, with all the right imaging and plenty of sequenced keyboards and drum programming to boot. But even on her 1992 *Real Life* debut, there was a hint of something greater beneath the surface. On that album's closing track, the touching and stark piano ballad "How Could I Ask for More," came a glimpse of the compelling songwriter that might one day emerge in all her glory.

We were not disappointed. Four years and three albums later, critics everywhere were entranced by the formidable *Listen*, a stunning exhibition of Morgan's vocal supremacy as well as her ability to give her common black-and-white piano keys a distinctive personality. Her stellar range never a question, Morgan lets loose with a verve and spirit that shakes foundations ("God Is Love") while also offering such vulnerability as to tingle any spine ("Need").

But producers Brent Bourgeois and Craig Hansen deserve a tip o' the hat, too, for giving Morgan the freedom every artist needs, while knowing just how to allow impeccably placed strings, woodwinds and percussion to enhance rather than distract from such a masterpiece. With no significant breaks between the tracks, the overall impression of *Listen* feels more like an event, an aural experience one can enjoy again and again.

—*April Hefner*

Exit/Island 1987
Produced by Robert Musso

77'S
SEVENTY SEVEN'S

82

Springing from the fertile ground of Sacramento, California's mission-to-the-mainstream Christian music scene (Charlie Peacock, Vector, Steve Scott, et al.), the Seventy Seven's hit the music biz in 1982 with its new wave-ish *Ping Pong Over the Abyss*, followed two years later by the more accomplished *All Fall Down*.

In 1987, however, the group had the support of mainstream powerhouse Island Records and were poised for stardom with 77's. But alas, it was not to be. (A record called *The Joshua Tree* kinda took Island's attention away.)

Nevertheless, 77's represents the band's most wide-ranging, memorable music, combining delicious pop melodies with barely restrained rock rhythms, leader Michael Roe's shimmering Stratocaster playing and plenty of lyrical and musical light and shade.

Songs like "Do It for Love"—with its "Born to Run" riff, Roe's unmistakable cry and catchy chorus—flow right into darker tunes like "I Can't Get Over It" and "Bottom Line," a beautifully succinct statement on human depravity. "The Lust, the Flesh, the Eyes & the Pride of Life"—with the Byrds' Chris Hillman on bass—is one of those melodies that upon first listen you swear you've heard before.

77's—the first of this brilliant band's eponymous albums—was the crown jewel in a career filled with gems still waiting to be discovered.

—*Dave Urbanski*

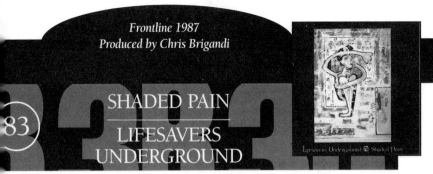

Frontline 1987
Produced by Chris Brigandi

SHADED PAIN

83

LIFESAVERS
UNDERGROUND

Lifesavers Underground © Shaded Pain

Michael Knott raged into the early '80s Southern California Christian music scene with a lethal combination of passion, artistry and weirdness, creating a rock band that changed its name and style as often as it needed to keep up with mainstream college-radio darlings.

But Knott & Co.'s 1987 release, *Shaded Pain*, was truly forward-looking. In fact, it became the standard bearer of "alternative" (*way* before the phrase became part of the cultural lexicon) and the touchstone for a generation of Christian bands since that aspired to hipness, vision and naked spirituality.

Here Knott combines the gothic, European vocal feel of then-current bands the Mission UK, the Sisters of Mercy and Echo and the Bunnymen with hard rock, punk and noisy guitar feedback à la the Jesus and Mary Chain (not bands or sounds Christian music listeners were used to then).

The lyrical borders are stretched as well, with Knott meeting the rough-and-tumble music with angry, anguished, downright depressing imagery. Titles like "Bye Bye Colour" and "Die Baby Die" conjure up death, as does "Our Time Has Come" with its "kiss the cleaver" verse. The finale, title track (an arresting, piano-only tune) names hurt, heartache and humanity as real aspects of the Christian experience before such introspection became commonplace.

—*Dave Urbanski*

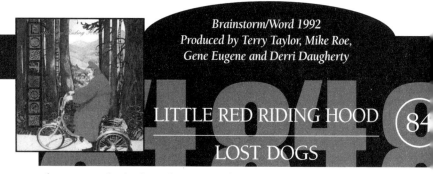

Brainstorm/Word 1992
Produced by Terry Taylor, Mike Roe,
Gene Eugene and Derri Daugherty

LITTLE RED RIDING HOOD ⑧④

LOST DOGS

The concept looked good on paper, but little did anyone know how good. In 1991, the front men from four of Christian music's most important and revered rock bands got together to form the Lost Dogs, a super-group of latent potential, one might say. Certainly inspired by the success two years earlier of the Dylan/Orbison/Petty/Lynne/Harrison combo The Travelling Wilburys, Terry Taylor (Daniel Amos, The Swirling Eddies), Gene Eugene (Adam Again), Michael Roe (The 77's) and Derri Daugherty (The Choir) formed a roots-rock side project that eclipsed their own bands in sales right out of the gate.

While the Dogs' debut, *Scenic Routes*, was certainly impressive in its bold embracing of country music as well as blues and pop, the follow-up *Little Red Riding Hood* proved the Dogs were more than an event—they were becoming a band. Though still compiled of Roe's edgy blues, Taylor and Daugherty's lilting country affections and Eugene's unmistakably world-weary presence, *Riding Hood* worked as a cohesive collection. Though probably best known for its radio hit "Pray Where You Are," the real soul of *Little Red Riding Hood* is best heard in songs like "No Ship Coming In," "Jimmy" and the hauntingly sparse "There's No Room for Us," not to mention the humorous bluegrass romp "Bad Indigestion."

—*John J. Thompson*

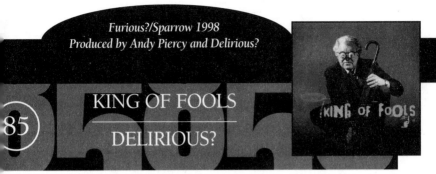

Furious?/Sparrow 1998
Produced by Andy Piercy and Delirious?

KING OF FOOLS
DELIRIOUS?

(85)

At the fore of the massive renewal movement among young European Christians in the mid-'90s was a humble quintet that started out playing original worship music for a tiny, once-a-month "Cutting Edge" youth group meeting in Littlehampton, England.

But things didn't stay small for long. Something was in the air—and Delirious? caught that "something" in its sails. The meetings were soon attracting 1,000 kids at a time. The band made some cassettes, played for 45,000 at Wembley Stadium and eventually recorded its first album, *King of Fools*. It debuted at number 13 on the British pop charts. This indie album caught the interest of Christian music types, and by 1998 Delirious? was the hottest, freshest band around. So much so that several of its songs became worship staples among American Gen-X churches ("Sanctify," "All the Way," "August 30th," "Hands of Kindness" and "What a Friend I've Found," among others).

Despite leader Martin Smith's slightly Bono-esque vocals (albeit with a cockney drawl) and the group's decidedly basic arrangements and melodies, *King of Fools* possesses unmistakable spiritual power. It is *the* songbook, the blueprint for what much of youth-oriented worship can and will be in the new millennium.

—*Dave Urbanski*

Myrrh 1996
Produced by Mark Heimermann

HEAVENLY PLACE
JACI VELASQUEZ

86

Discovered after opening a Point of Grace show and then quickly ushered into the recording studio, 16-year-old Jaci Velasquez dive bombed into the Christian music scene like no artist ever before. Her first album, *Heavenly Place*, blew up crazy, becoming the fastest selling debut by a solo artist in the history of Christian music to date.

What's more, before Ricky Martin and Jennifer Lopez became flavors of the month, Velasquez's smooth, Latin-flavored pop became a mainstay on the radio charts, with five *Heavenly Place* singles shooting straight to number one. And with her pretty face splashed across TV screens and magazine covers, it was no surprise when Velasquez took the Dove Award for New Artist of the Year.

But the superior sounds on *Heavenly Place* would have been enough for any listener to take notice. Besides Mark Heimermann's experienced production hand and the high quality of the ten songs, one of the main reasons *Heavenly Place* stands out is Velasquez's spot-on vocal interpretations. Though she cowrote only one song, Velasquez invokes her confident, worldly-wise pipes and makes each song sound like a part of her very being. And no amount of record label cash can buy that kind of talent.

—*Dave Urbanski*

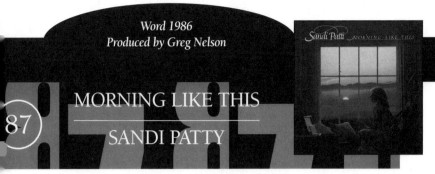

Word 1986
Produced by Greg Nelson

MORNING LIKE THIS

SANDI PATTY

87

Morning Like This, Sandi Patty's eighth album in the seven years since her 1979 debut, raised the standard previously set with the platinum selling, award-winning *Hymns Just for You* (1985). With *Morning Like This*, this orchestrated, inspirational *tour de force* captured Patty's first solo Grammy for Best Female Gospel Performance and six Dove Awards—two for Gospel Artist of the Year ('87, '88), two for Female Vocalist of the Year ('87,'88), Inspirational Album of the Year in '87 and cowriter of 1988's Song of the Year, "In the Name of the Lord." Simply put, *Morning Like This* established Patty (then Patti) as the undisputed queen of inspirational music.

And with a collection of songs this outstanding, it's no wonder. "Let There Be Praise," "Love in Any Language," "In the Name of the Lord" and "There Is a Savior" not only climbed up the inspirational charts but also found their way into Sunday morning worship all across the country. Sandi Patty's distinctively beautiful voice—think opera-meets-gospel-meets-Broadway with an unbelievable range—impressed audiences nationwide. And doors from the White House to *The Tonight Show* continued to open in the years that followed.

As a testament to the strength and beauty of *Morning Like This*, the songs are still popular church favorites more than a decade after the album's release.

—*Melissa Riddle*

Enigma 1986
Produced by Stephan Galfas, Michael Sweet,
Robert Sweet and Oz Fox

TO HELL WITH THE DEVIL

STRYPER

88

With heavy Top 40 airplay and massive support from MTV for the video to "Honestly," Orange County, California-based Stryper's third release, *To Hell with the Devil*, marked the platinum-selling pinnacle of its memorable career.

Earning the group a Grammy nomination, *To Hell with the Devil* thrust Stryper—Michael Sweet (vocals, guitar), Oz Fox (guitar, vocals), Timothy Gaines (bass) and Robert Sweet (drums)—into both widespread appeal and controversy. The glam-rock foursome pushed the boundaries of what Christian music could look and sound like—and to whom religious rock might appeal outside of the traditional Christian fan base. On *To Hell with the Devil*, Stryper's cocktail of heavy, arena rock guitar, screaming confessional lyrics— and the occasional splash of sensitive balladry, as on "Honestly"— decidedly gave notice to bands like Motley Crue and Judas Priest: to hell with your devil.

1990's *Against the Law* broke a two-year self-imposed retreat from music in the midst of internal and public controversy. Sporting a new sound and new, less-glamorous image, the album flopped, and the band split, as Michael Sweet left Stryper to pursue a solo career with the Benson label.

—*Gregory Rumburg*

Produced by R. Kelly, B-Rite 1998, A-Tone,
Stan Scates, Big Yam, Victor Merritt, Kevin Bond,
Buster & Shavoni, Percy Bady, Soulshock & Karlin
and Laythan Armor

89

TRIN-I-TEE 5:7
TRIN-I-TEE 5:7

As Trin-i-tee 5:7 revamped the idea of female soul gospel singing to glamorous new ends, the threesome offered a chaste alternative on their debut album to distaff R&B groups more willing to exploit their sexuality to sell their songs. That dual concept worked to stunning effect.

A remake of the classic "Oh Mary, Don't You Weep" proved the gals could *sang* as if they walked from a muggy storefront church directly to the recording studio. The album's biggest recipient of mainstream R&B airplay, "God's Grace," tempered all that soulfulness to a lyric by conflicted urban lover man R. Kelly.

Per the norm for R&B and dance albums of the day, the group engaged in the occasional skit, too. "Saved Boy" asserted that Christian singles could have their eyes on prospective mates while remembering that it's what's in their spirits that counts most.

Even as the trio earned a gold sales plaque for *Trin-i-tee 5:7*, the trio has seen little imitation or competition. The unspoken sentiment may be to not mess with an entity that fills its niches so sublimely. Trin-i-tee 5:7 does just that.

—Jamie Lee Rake

Frontline 1990
Produced by Jon Gibson

JESUS LOVES YA
JON GIBSON

90

Jon Gibson had already made an impact in Christian music circles with a couple of albums that established him as a soul singer with a hunger. With *Jesus Loves Ya*, Gibson's artistic and commercial appetites paid off with an album that flowed with high, effortless cool. It gave him a deep mine of radio hits and a sales smash.

With poppingly rubbery bass and a stroll beat playing beneath Gibson's Stevie Wonder-ful vocals with their "Hallelujah" 's, scat singing and simple lyrics, "Jesus Loves Ya" was a natural. Christian radio programmers and listeners had the good sense to make it huge.

The sunny tone kept on in the semiautobiographical "Love Come Down" and "Tequila." On the soul/rock ballad "Everlasting," Gibson shined with equal brightness when getting into more forceful funk. On "Enough's Enough," a duet with M. C. Peace 586, and "Straight One," the more stringent grooves bring out songs of warning and confrontation.

After another chart-topping album, *Forever Friends*, Gibson would fall into label deals that failed to meet the challenge of his expanding sonic palette. *Jesus Loves Ya* captured Gibson at an optimally soulful moment.

—*Jamie Lee Rake*

Star Song 1978
Produced by Resurrection Band

AWAITING YOUR REPLY

91

RESURRECTION BAND

If the Christian music industry was slow to embrace rock and pop music that sounded like what was hip on the Top 40, that reluctance fossilized in response to hard rock and metal. Petra may have been the first real rock band on a Christian label, but its early albums were limited by bad production that exhibited a fear of the two things that matter most in this genre: drums and guitars. Ever an independent evangelistic outreach of the Jesus People, U.S.A. community in Chicago, Resurrection Band was free to do what it knew was best, thus *Awaiting Your Reply* was a real hard rock album with a real hard rock sound.

Glenn Kaiser's gritty, soulful vocals and tendency toward big guitar riff driven blues/rock songs in the vibe of Led Zeppelin and Black Sabbath would capture the imagination of metal heads who were unimpressed by most Christian pop. Rez Band would lead a host of young metal bands into a space where creative music and bold Christian witness coalesced. Later, J.P.U.S.A. would host the Cornerstone Festival, giving further encouragement and providing a place where Christian hard and alternative music acts and their fans could come together.

Amazingly, songs like "Waves," "Broken Promises," "Light Shine" and "Irish Garden" stand the test of time.

—*Brian Quincy Newcomb*

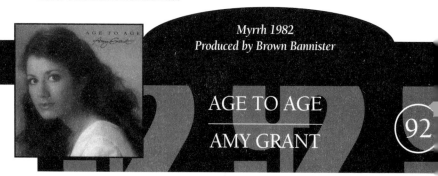

Myrrh 1982
Produced by Brown Bannister

AGE TO AGE

AMY GRANT

92

In light of what would follow (the maturity of *Lead Me On*, the MTV-ready pop of *Heart in Motion* or the unsettling honesty of *Behind the Eyes*), 1982's *Age to Age* can't help but seem somewhat quaint. By today's standards it's hardly hip; in fact, this incarnation of Amy Grant seems positively prim compared to the leopard-print version that would emerge only two albums later. But the production, helmed by Brown Bannister, was a huge step up from other Christian recordings of the day.

More importantly, nearly two decades after its release, classics like "El Shaddai," written by Michael Card and John Thompson, and the Rich Mullins-penned "Sing Your Praise to the Lord" hold their own against current worship favorites (Kathy Troccoli and an unknown named Michael W. Smith also pitched in on the project). The collaborations between Grant and her then-new husband, Gary Chapman, are also refreshing in the simple faith of their lyrics. Out of the whole bunch, only "Fat Baby" seems a misstep, but even it has its charms, reminding us of a time when Amy Grant was young and naïve enough to find a song like this or "Grape, Grape Joy" funny.

Age to Age may not be the first CD you reach for when wanting an "Amy fix," but remember, this made the music that followed it possible. And as a tribute to its longevity, there are those who are *still* waiting for Grant to make another just like it.

—*Wendy Lee Nentwig*

Myrrh 1977
Produced by Buck Herring

HOW THE WEST WAS ONE

(93)

THE 2ND CHAPTER OF ACTS, PHIL KEAGGY AND "A BAND CALLED DAVID"

The friendly, familial atmosphere surrounding *How the West Was One* camouflaged an epic, gutsy commercial and artistic move for Christian music. As the market's second live album (following a set by Barry McGuire), two of the relatively young scene's acts to be considered "stars" were teamed up with a solid ad hoc backing band over the course of a triple-LP set.

On the cusp of the 2nd Chapter's increased bent toward adult-contemporary blandness, *One* showcased them as a rather eclectically rocking unit, too. "Hey, Watcha Say" references disco's thump, while "Easter Song" recounts the Resurrection with a madrigal lilt. Those Ward kids had a way with an anthem or two as well, as proven by "Which Way the Wind Blows" and "Yaweh," among others.

For Keaggy fans, only fan club albums and concert appearances find him working his muse in extended jams more than he does here. "What a Day," "Rejoice," "Time" and the autobiographical "My Life" give his mellifluous guitar plenty of breathing room.

Christian music's increased profitability has probably, ironically, rendered albums daring as *How the West Was One* remote possibilities these days, even were they to team up acts of commensurate contemporary appeal as that of Keaggy and 2nd Chapter then.

—*Jamie Lee Rake*

Warner Alliance 1991
Produced by Brown Bannister

MICHAEL ENGLISH
MICHAEL ENGLISH

94

When Warner Alliance put their money on Southern gospel veteran Michael English, it was as safe a bet as one can make. After all, English's *GQ* face and powerhouse tenor voice matched with producer Brown Bannister and radio-magic songs is the formula for sure success. English's self-titled solo debut did not disappoint.

A solid adult contemporary mix of dance pop and blue-eyed soul, *Michael English* jumped to the top of the Christian radio charts with "Solid As the Rock," and "In Christ Alone," a stunning ballad that revealed the stellar vocal gift of this 28-year-old Wallace, North Carolina, native. "Mary, Did You Know?" since recorded by a bevy of artists in Christian and mainstream music, landed in the top five.

The album not only introduced English to the contemporary Christian music world, it catapulted the small-town boy to the head of the line, taking both "New Artist of the Year" and "Male Vocalist of the Year" at the 1992 Dove Awards—no small feat for any singer. Even music critics of the day heralded *Michael English* as a classic, "What people had in mind when they originally thought of contemporary Christian music—an inspiring, rousing message infused with the best that music has to offer in its day" (*CCM*, November 1991).

This was the first shooting star of the decade, at his brightest and best.

—*Melissa Riddle*

Lamb & Lion 1979
Produced by Joseph Hardy, Eddie DeGarmo
and Dana Key

STRAIGHT ON

DEGARMO & KEY

95

Eddie DeGarmo and Dana Key were boyhood friends who grew up in the shadow of Graceland in Memphis. Forming their first band when they were in sixth grade, the two were influenced by Delta blues and rock. After coming to Christ in their late teens, the focus of their music shifted, and they eventually released 15 Christian albums as DeGarmo & Key before disbanding in the mid '90s.

Straight On was D&K's second album on Pat Boone's Lamb & Lion label—a powerful follow-up to their promising debut. It was an immediate standout because it represented a standard-setting quantum leap in production quality. D&K was one of the few groups at the time to display authentic rock 'n' roll attitude with production that was musically right in tune with the synth-driven arena rock of the day.

Long instrumental introductions reminiscent of Styx or Boston added an artful flair, and Dana Key's earnest vocals gave the songs an edge rarely heard in the Christian rock of the day. "Go Tell Them," "Livin' on the Edge of Dyin'" and "Mary" are standout cuts.

—*John W. Styll*

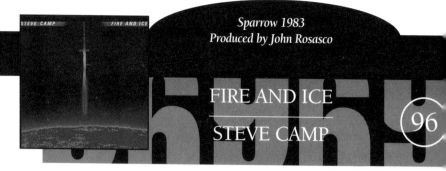

Sparrow 1983
Produced by John Rosasco

FIRE AND ICE
STEVE CAMP

96

Known now as a bit of a firebrand since he "nailed" the Christian music world in 1997 with his 107 Theses (a letter outlining where he felt the industry had strayed from God's will), back in 1983 Steve Camp was one of the true up-and-comers in the Christian pop scene. Though he debuted in the late '70s under the tutelage of Larry Norman, it was on this, his debut for Sparrow, that Camp first achieved Christian "star" status.

By utilizing a formula that saw a certain number of "rock" songs (the title cut, "Squeeze," and the bold "Upon This Rock") to appeal to the kids, a few "radio" songs ("Living in Laodicea" became an enduring fan favorite but "Love's Not a Feeling," the duet with Michelle Pillar, was the runaway radio hit in its day) and a good bunch of midtempo pop tunes, Camp managed to please a pretty wide range of fans with *Fire and Ice.*

Lyrically Camp's theological perspectives start to come through here, and the title cut in tandem with "Laodicea" create an all-or-nothing approach to living out faith. Camp was as bold with his words as he was with his hooks. Many feel that *Fire and Ice* was his high point as a rock singer, something he would stray from in years to come.

—*John J. Thompson*

Metro One 1993
Produced by Brian Ray

THE BRIDE
CRYSTAL LEWIS

THE BRIDE

CRYSTAL LEWIS

97

Crystal Lewis had been blowing away listeners with her fulsome, versatile pipes since her mid-1980s teenage stint with punkabilly outfit Wild Blue Yonder. Since embarking on her solo career, the question surrounding Lewis has always been how to market a voice capable of doing exquisitely whatever its owner set out to do with it. On *The Bride*, the dilemma was answered by Lewis' producer/husband letting her darn well do what she wanted.

It worked to a dazzlingly eclectic effect. Between an opening Brazilian-flavored jazz salvo on "Don't Worry" and a concluding *a cappella* rendition of "Amazing Grace," her aesthetic explorations made simultaneous sense as both a showcase for her awesome vocal gift and components of a loosely defined concept album. "Little Jackie" 's funky acid jazz complements her gospel side on "The Mother and the Bride" and "Holy Place." The anthemic inspirational bombast surrounding her take on "My Redeemer Lives" effectively plays against her deliciously blues rockin' "You'll Be Back for Me." And her jaw-dropping vocal on the after-hours cabaret jazz arrangement of "Jesus Belongs in Your Heart" served notice that this pint-sized powerhouse had chops head and shoulders above most all the rest.

—*Jamie Lee Rake*

Star Song 1982
Produced by Jonathan David Brown

MORE POWER TO YA

PETRA

98

Being the premier rock band in Christian music of the early '80s, Petra aspired not only to minister to its young listeners, but also to make albums that answered the quality of general market counterparts such as Journey and Foreigner. The arrangements and production of 1982's *More Power to Ya* didn't quite attain the quality of the aforementioned groups, but this record—if nothing else—pointed the way toward what Christian rock *could* attain sonically.

There's still no doubting Petra's collective playing and singing abilities, however. The guys are note-perfect and watertight from beginning to end, drenching the whole project with their signature, multipart vocal harmonies.

But the true strength of *More Power to Ya*, and what keeps it vibrant today, is its completely God-focused lyrics. The conviction behind Bob Hartman's pen and Greg X. Volz's tireless tenor may sound dated only because hardly any artist sings about such simple, uncompromising faith anymore.

The opener, "Stand Up," calls on Christians to walk their talks; the acoustic "Road to Zion" points believers toward heaven (and would stick around youth-group worship for years); and "Judas Kiss" drips with bloody guilt over sin. No group before or since could put a Bible study to music like Petra.

—*Dave Urbanski*

Myrrh 1986
Produced by Keith Thomas

THE CHAMPION

(99)

CARMAN

The enigma that is Carman Licciardello is one of those pop music mysteries for the record books. Like Grand Funk Railroad, Kenny G, Vanilla Ice and a hundred more like them, Carman's fans fill football stadiums and make cash registers ring, thoroughly enjoying a phenomenon that keeps critics, most of whom don't share the fans' enthusiasm, scratching their heads.

The Champion is a landmark for Carman, because it introduced us to the title track that is his showpiece. "The Champion" depicts a celestial boxing match between Jesus and Satan with God the Father as the referee. Satan tells Jesus he is "dead meat" to which our Lord replies, "Go ahead, make my day." Jesus eventually hits the canvas, but of course rises up victorious before the count of ten is complete to gain the eternal heavyweight championship title. This number one-charting song encompasses everything you either loved or loathed about Carman.

The album also included an early praise anthem in "Revive Us Oh Lord" (which reached number four), and the artist is listed as writer or cowriter of every track. And for the record, Carman was one of the first Christian artists to hit gold and platinum sales levels without the necessity of crossing over to the pop mainstream.

—Robert Mineo

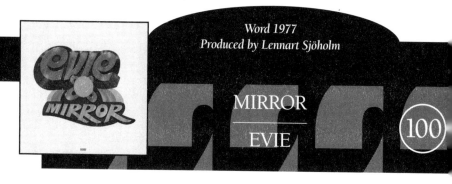

Word 1977
Produced by Lennart Sjöholm

MIRROR
EVIE

(100)

Before there was Amy or Sandi, there was Evie. Evie Tornquist was an American-born singer whose Scandinavian heritage allowed her to make records in Sweden as well as in the States. On her first album for Word in 1974, Evie covered the top songs by the emerging contemporary Christian and gospel artists of the period like Andraé Crouch and Larry Norman, albeit with a lighter musical touch. By 1977, three more albums had been released (one in Swedish), and they were received with the kind of acceptance and radio airplay to warrant calling her Christian music's first "star."

Mirror was her biggest success to date, an album that exhibited her maturity as an interpreter of the album's mostly original songs far beyond the pixie image that had worked well for her earlier on. Producer Lennart Sjöholm added more complex arrangements to the generally upbeat program to take the singer into deeper territory. Today's ears would label this "inspirational," but *Mirror* was the standard for Christian pop at the time...though Amy Grant's first album would be released later that same year.

—Thom Granger

HONORABLE MENTIONS

As I stated in the Introduction, it's very possible you won't find some of your favorite Christian albums in this book. I should add that many of the writers that contributed to the poll and to this book didn't see some of their favorites make the cut either. It's the nature of the thing, of course, but we thought it might be fun to let some of the writers (present company included) name a few of their personal best that didn't make the list, and why they feel those albums are some of the greatest. Enjoy.

Anthony DeBarros

Mercury/THE PRAYER CHAIN—Layers of psychedelic guitar textures and ambient noises make this one of Christian music's most artful successes.

_____

Way Back Home/PHIL KEAGGY—The guitar master turns his attention to the joys of family, creating a poignant set of acoustic-driven songs.

_____

At the Foot of the Cross, Vol. 1: Clouds, Rain, Fire—This early '90s production by The Choir's Steve Hindalong and Derri Daugherty and a host of players is the spiritual progenitor of dozens of modern worship albums.

_____

Art of the State/AD—Former Kansas leader Kerry Livgren creates a small-scale progressive rock masterpiece, fusing keyboard-driven rock with artful compositions.

_____

Tales of Wonder/WHITE HEART—Arena rock at its best, a reminder of the days when big hooks, big guitars and sparkling harmonies ruled the airwaves.

_____

Thom Granger

Perfecta/ADAM AGAIN—Desperately sad and unblinkingly truthful, this amazing band's last completed album was my favorite. I will always be grateful for the gifts of Gene Eugene.

_____

Blue Plate Special (general market version)/RICK ALTIZER—This ridiculously talented *wunderkind* hasn't had his 15 minutes of fame yet, but I can say I heard him first.

_____

Ceili Rain/CEILI RAIN—Veteran pop songwriter Bob Halligan Jr. nailed his theses to the wall of an Irish pub in this brilliant Celtic-flavored manifesto of life and love in the Spirit.

_____

You Gotta Sin to Get Saved/MARIA MCKEE—Former Lone Justice front woman infuses every track here with her intelligence, compassion and foundational spirituality.

_____

Achtung Baby/U2—The album and tour of the decade for me, U2 chronicled the dissolution of a marriage with majestic music, lyrics almost unbearably intimate and surprisingly inspirational.

———

LAURA HARRIS

The Basic Stuff/BILLY CROCKETT—This acoustic album combined the amenities of the studio with the feel of live performance, subsequently becoming a soundtrack for worshipers and revelers all over America.

———

Brave Heart/KIM HILL—The pinnacle of Hill's stint as one of Christian music's premiere folk/rock chicks, this disc left large footprints that many girls with guitars have subsequently followed in.

———

Wakened By the Wind/SUSAN ASHTON—Ashton and Wayne Kirkpatrick took their maiden voyages together on this project (she as an artist, he as a producer), and the resulting musical purity, freshness and innocence defies duplication.

———

Making Light of It/PIERCE PETTIS—Pettis' outstanding songwriting is a standard that others in the industry would do well to measure themselves by.

———

The Jesus Record/RICH MULLINS AND A RAGAMUFFIN BAND—Producer Rick Elias and the rest of the Ragamuffins fulfilled Mullins' last work with passion and precision, a feat that rendered these songs death-defying.

———

APRIL HEFNER

Night of Your Return/FERNANDO ORTEGA—As an independent CD, it was difficult to argue for the inclusion of this one on our final list of 100. While Ortega's voice and songs are so beautiful, so rich, so moving that it would make sense for all of his albums to appear, this project—the first of his I'd heard—will always hold a special place.

———

Time/THIRD DAY—The third time's the charm for Southern rockers Third Day with a CD that boasts excellent production (courtesy of Monroe Jones) that finally captures the band's live energy and immense charisma.

Freedom/WHITE HEART—The discussions were intense, but *Freedom* lost out to *Don't Wait for the Movie* in the final analysis. For me, *Freedom* will always be the White Heart disc with the best collection of songs.

Curious/JAN KRIST—Who? That's the response of most Christian music fans, but Krist is a writer and musician not to be overlooked for her poetic, thoughtful work, and *Curious* is her best studio representation of that to date.

I 2 Eye/MICHAEL W. SMITH—Yes, Smitty's other three selections on the Greatest 100 list are fine choices, but this one evokes too many tender high school memories to be overlooked.

Robert Mineo

See Inside/OUT OF THE GREY— Just when you thought the Dentes may have been in a rut, they delivered a great set of muscular, organic pop featuring keepers like "Disappear" and "Not a Chance."

Sleep Sound in Jesus/MICHAEL CARD—Long before "Butterfly Kisses," Michael Card created a wonderful set of simple yet scripturally profound lullabies that remain some of the most cherished ties that bind in my own household.

Live the Life/MICHAEL W. SMITH—A personal favorite of Smitty's more recent "grown up" work includes his best cut ever, "Missing Person," and other well-realized goodies like the Eurodisco "I Believe in You Now" and the psychedelic title track anthem.

Falling Forward/MARGARET BECKER—Like the Dentes, Maggie B. also snapped herself back to attention with a moody, passionate and very smart piece of progressive adult pop.

Wide Eyed/NICHOLE NORDEMAN—One of the best, most original debuts ever, packed with intelligence, vulnerability, melodic invention and sharp observation.

BRIAN Q. NEWCOMB

Now Do You Understand?/RANDY MATTHEWS—One of the early veterans of Christian rock, Matthews is my hero. He literally laid down his life and career for his friends, and the truth of the gospel and the power of this music. As artful as it was groundbreaking, these songs, poetry and stories shaped my early faith in profound ways…and not just because I was one of the "weird ones" sitting down front when it was recorded at my alma mater, Houghton College, which was so repulsed by the radical content that they asked to be left off the disc's credits.

Stealing Fire/BRUCE COCKBURN—There's deep spirituality and vulnerable humanity, a prophet's cry and a poet's heart at work in "Lovers in a Dangerous Time," "Making Contact," "To Raise the Morning Star," "Nicaragua" and even the controversial "If I Had a Rocket Launcher," but it's "Maybe the Poet" with its summary of Galatians 3:28's impressive inclusivity that touches me most deeply.

Truth Decay/T-BONE BURNETT—As with the Cockburn record above, Burnett wrote about the real world we share in the light of God's loving awareness. "Power of Love" may be the perfect pop gospel song, and this guy's influence on Christian artistry has been underrated for far too long.

Killing Floor/VIGILANTES OF LOVE—My first introduction to songwriter Bill Mallonee struck the deepest, here produced by Mark Heard. From the promising pop single "Real Down Town" to the honest hymnody of "Earth Has No Sorrow (Heaven Can't Heal)," and great slices of humanity like "Anybody's Guess," "Motel Room," "Deep End" and "Sick of It All," I felt as if I'd been joined by a fellow traveler who would sing my life back to me.

Scenic Routes/LOST DOGS—The first time collaboration of these front men is still my favorite. It's chock-full of folky, country spirit and great performances, plus the original version of "Breathe Deep, the Breath of God"—again an anthem of the inclusive character of God's redeeming love...I'm beginning to detect a theme here.

———

DWIGHT OZARD

A Love Supreme/JOHN COLTRANE—for its daring musicality and seamless commitment to finding a way to express a broken man's certain faith.

———

JAMIE LEE RAKE

The Lyrical Strength of One Street Poet/D-BOY—Puerto Rican-American rapper makes great creative strides on second album before being gunned down.

———

LeVoyage/SANDI PATTY—Inspirational diva comes closest she has yet to fulfilling her Broadway musical-starring dreams with this satisfying concept album recorded during her messy divorce.

———

The Gift of Tears/THE REVOLUTIONARY ARMY OF THE INFANT JESUS—Medieval chant, *musique concrete,* disco, progressive English folk rock and plenty else intertwine on debut album from criminally obscure Brit iconoclasts.

———

Low Estate/16 HORSEPOWER—Southern Gothicism (from Denver!) rife with sin, salvation and bracing acoustic arrangements makes for the most alternative of alt country.

———

Kickin'/THE MIGHTY CLOUDS OF JOY—Joe Ligon & Co.'s most commercially successful foray into soul gospel/disco fusion is representative as any of the sub-genre to birth today's sanctified dance music movement.

———

JOHN J. THOMPSON

Art of the State/KERRY LIVGREN AND AD—Kerry Livgren brought a much-needed dose of artistry and intricacy to the Christian rock scene with all of his releases.

———

Reconciled/THE CALL—The Call brought inspirational lyrics and a fresh breath of passion and faith into the college rock scene in the early to mid-'80s. *Reconciled* features "I Still Believe" (which has been covered by Russ Taff) and "Everywhere I Go."

Zionic Bonds/ANDY MCCARROLL AND MORAL SUPPORT—Back in 1982, Andy McCarroll obviously didn't know the rules about not using the latest, most cutting edge music to drive home a Christian message. *Zionic Bonds* is full-throttle post-punk rock with the sneer of Johnny Rotten and the zeal of Glenn Kaiser all rolled into one.

ATF/AFTER THE FIRE—After over a decade of releasing experimental art-rock, the members of After the Fire finally had a smash hit with 1984's "Der Kommissar" (a cover of a Falco tune). Unfortunately the band had already broken up by the time *ATF* was released in the states, but their faith-informed keyboard rock was hugely influential nonetheless.

Light Maneuvers/SERVANT—Servant was right up there with Petra in the early days of Christian rock. *Light Maneuvers,* with killer production by Bob Rock, scored a major hit with "We Are the Light" and managed to rock out far more than most CHR records that year.

Sunday's Child/PHIL KEAGGY—*Sunday's Child* brought the amazing talents of Phil Keaggy together with the musicianship of some of the best in the biz (Rick Cua, Randy Stonehill, Derri Daugherty, Russ Taff, Mike Mead, Tim Chandler, David Miner) and the songwriting of Mark Heard, Russ Taff and others. In my opinion, *Sunday's Child* is THE classic rock record in Christian music.

DAVE URBANSKI

Chagall Guevara/CHAGALL GUEVARA—A general market, alt-rock, critically acclaimed album by Christian music's finest. Steve Taylor's thickly veiled lyrics are full of spiritual insight, wit and sarcasm; the dream band's fiery chops are first-rate, mature and complex. Sadly, their shooting-star magic lasted but a few months. (How 'bout a reunion, guys?)

Vinyl Confessions/KANSAS—Longtime singer Steve Walsh quit the band after refusing to sing "Crossfire," Kerry Livgren's most explicitly evangelistic tune to date—a tumultuous beginning-of-the-end for the veteran prog rockers. But even more, this artful, excellently produced album revealed to tons of Kansas fans where Livgren's soul search finally ended.

Squint/STEVE TAYLOR—A post grunge, diverse, crackerjack of a record that shines on every front. Taylor's disgust with the church ("Smug," "Easy Listening," "The Moshing Floor") is tempered by encouragement ("Jesus Is for Losers," "The Finish Line") and a hilarious-yet-heavy finale, "Cash Cow."

Lament/THE RESURRECTION BAND—The fruits of King's X axeman Ty Tabor's production are all over this neo-rock opera (listen especially to the tasty chorus of top-charting single, "Summerthrow"), and they catapult Rez back into the metal heaven where Glenn Kaiser & Co. belong. Touching, profound, and real.

The Wind and the Wheat/PHIL KEAGGY—This Grammy winner is one of the most memorable, evocative electric-guitar dominated instrumental albums I've ever heard. At once soothing and powerful, Keaggy's compositions paint vivid, emotional pictures and still sound fresh and moving today.

CHRIS WILLMAN

Upon This Rock/LARRY NORMAN—Blatantly evangelistic, unapologetically eschatological and occasionally surreal, this was arguably the first real Christian rock album, and not a bad start for the genre at all. He still wishes we'd all been ready.

So Long Ago the Garden/LARRY NORMAN—Trilogy, schmilogy! Who cares if it took a grand, overarching concept for Norman to justify writing material this dark and this good. (Bonus points for being the only Christian album ever to reference 1940s actor "Guy Kibbee, who was dead.")

Saved/BOB DYLAN—Even diehard secularists now agree they underrated Dylan's second "born again" album, Zimmy's straight-up—albeit rockin'—take on black gospel, which offered possibly the most heartfelt and expressive croaking of his career.

Tribal Opera/IDEOLA—Mark Heard was known as a roots guy before and after, but this one-man-band effort found him treading techno-rock territory and reaching some emotional peaks amid the machinery. Childhood-lost highlight: the epic-sounding "How to Grow Up Big and Strong."

Reconciled/THE CALL—Michael Been is a master of barely controlled passion, and no rocker ever sounded more frustrated by worldly weights and hungrier for God than the guy singing "Everywhere I Go" and "I Still Believe," two great moments in rock 'n' roll Christendom.

AFTERWORD

John Fischer

Christian music as art? Christian music as a cultural influence? Christian music as great music, regardless of its time and place? These attributes have been present in Christian music from the beginning, but not always recognized. The albums in this collection give credence to the notion that music written, recorded and performed by Christians can be judged as much on the basis of its artistic merit and its universal themes as by its Christianity.

Throughout the course of its brief history, Christian music as art has often been eclipsed by Christian music as ministry. These two have even been in conflict. Many have feuded over these designations and insisted on exempting Christian music from evaluation and review. In the end, it all depends on how one views the Christian as an artist.

If the Christian artist is the receptacle of a special anointing of God for a specific ministry to a generation, then it is hard to take issue with the vehicle of expression. If God has touched the lips of the singer/songwriter with the hot coal of his holy blessing, who are we to challenge the artistic merit of that which pours forth? "Thus saith the Lord" leaves no room for evaluation.

In the early days of Christian music, this way of thinking was prevalent. The songwriting process was held in awe. The word "anointed" was often used to describe the music that best moved the listener. Indeed, "anointed" became synonymous with "good." In an attempt at humility, the direct hand of God upon the artist was evoked and the music was treated almost like Scripture—as directly handed down by God. The best songs took the least effort. The artist was merely the scribe.

In spite of this thinking, there were those Christians who worked hard at their craft. They saw themselves as frail human beings seeking to chronicle their own spiritual journey in ways that would reflect the honesty of their soul-struggle. For these people, the creative process was not so simple. Like a sculptor chiseling something recognizable out of nothing but stone, their Christianity was the motivation that kept them seeking the presence of God in their work and the hand of God in their lives. God did not move the chisel and hammer—they did—but God became the reason and the goal of all the hammering. They sought to give expression to the form of God that was present all along in the stone, but not revealed without the artist's eye and steady hand.

For these artists, the thing that birthed them and gave them a platform at times became their adversary. Christian music came with great expectations. The music was not going to express the soul of a Christian as much as it was going to make converts, save souls and entertain believers who wanted to stay current with their culture without having to endure its non-Christian bias. The demands of a Christian subculture and a growing Christian market have at times shut out the voices of the real artists among us.

Having been involved with the movement of Christian music from its inception in the late '60s, I have gone through periods when I have manifested, in my own artistic journey, both these perspectives. I know I still have, even today, a tendency to romanticize the early days of my career. In my memory, it does seem that my first songs sort of fell out of heaven. After that, it seemed, I had to work at it. I can remember wondering if it was okay to review albums in *CCM* magazine. Do we review people's ministries? How can you judge an album as bad art if even one soul was saved as the result of it? But then I began to explore my own artistic nature and discovered that as an artist, I was not a prophet delivering God's word as much as one who bares his own soul. Though the words are mine, God is somehow present in them in much the same way as he is present in me. It is a mystery. "Continue to work out your salvation with fear and trembling, for it is God who works in you..." (Philippians 2:12,13). Such a statement from the apostle Paul takes on great significance for the Christian artist and also makes the Christian artist an illustration of the normal Christian life. For the work of finding God in human experience, I believe, is the work of every Christian.

By now you may have noted that some of the artists in this collection are not the big Christian superstars you would expect in such an elite grouping of talent. Some paid a price for what they deemed "artistic integrity" when more explicitly Christian songs would have gained them greater attention in the Christian market. But they had their eye on more than success. They had their eye on the mystery of God hidden in the failures, disappointments and inequities of human existence. They explored the deeper questions of life—the gray areas in the midst of a black and white culture—and they used their artistic endeavors to do so. We are indebted to them, and especially to those in this collection who are no longer with us in body but left their legacy behind.

Many thanks to the artists who struggled to pass their work on to us and to those with the wisdom to notice. Perhaps with this in mind, we can all live our Christian lives with more of a creative eye— looking, like the sculptor, to cut God's presence out of the hard stone of our daily temporal existence.

John Fischer was a pioneering Christian singer/songwriter in the late '60s and early '70s, but is best known these days as an author and speaker whose monthly column has been the "last word" in *CCM* magazine for more years than we can count. It seemed only fitting that he grant that same benediction to this collection of essays on the music he helped create.

ARTIST INDEX

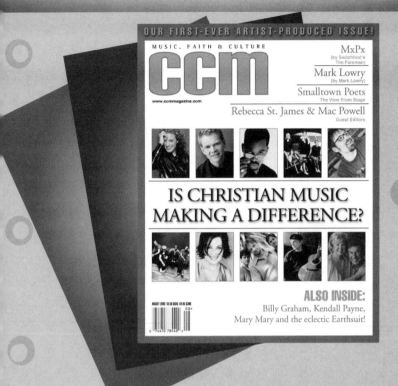